Selecting School Leaders

Guidelines for Making Tough Decisions

William R. Holland

Rowman & Littlefield Education
Lanham, Maryland • Toronto • Oxford
2006

Published in the United States of America
by Rowman & Littlefield Education
A Division of Rowman & Littlefield Publishers, Inc.
A wholly owned subsidary of The Rowman & Littlefield Publishing Group, Inc.
4501 Forbes Boulevard, Suite 200, Lanham, Maryland 20706
www.rowmaneducation.com

PO Box 317
Oxford
OX2 9RU, UK

Although this book was inspired by actual events in the author's life, it is a book of
fiction where the names, characters, places, and incidents are the product of the
author's imagination or are used fictitiously.

British Library Cataloguing in Publication Information Available

Library of Congress Cataloging-in-Publication Data

Holland, William R., 1938–
    Selecting school leaders : guidelines for making tough decisions / William R.
Holland.
        p.   cm.
    Includes bibliographical references.
    ISBN-13: 978-1-57886-487-4 (hardcover : alk. paper)
    ISBN-10: 1-57886-487-9 (hardcover : alk. paper)
    ISBN-13: 978-1-57886-488-1 (pbk. : alk. paper)
    ISBN-10: 1-57886-488-7 (pbk. : alk. paper)
        1. School principals—Selection and appointment—United States.   2. School
management and organization—United States.   I. Title.
    LB2831.952.H65   2006
    371.2'012—dc22
                                                                                2006007107

∞ ™ The paper used in this publication meets the minimum requirements of
American National Standard for Information Sciences—Permanence of
Paper for Printed Library Materials, ANSI/NISO Z39.48-1992.

Manufactured in the United States of America.

To my wife, Karen, my daughter, Kathy,
and my sons, Kevin and Steven,
for their patience, encouragement, and support.

Contents

Foreword

Today, as the nation completes the transition to an economy based on knowledge, the role of school administrators is more important than ever. It is abundantly clear that America's position in the world marketplace is now highly dependent on the quality of education in our schools. As the leaders of those schools, principals and superintendents have the responsibility for continual improvement toward that end, raising the bar for teachers, students, and communities. At the same time, they are asked to accomplish these goals with constrained resources and hard scrutiny of the use of those resources. Their lives are not, as we say in Rhode Island, a day at the beach!

The forces that swirl around the leaders of our schools are myriad. We live in a time where, paradoxically, change is our only constant. And that change accelerates in geometric, not arithmetic, progressions. The new brain sciences are teaching us much more about how our students learn. Our sons and daughters are "wired in" to new information and communication technology in ways that amaze and bewilder many of us. The latest wave of immigration to America is changing the social and political institutions with which we were once comfortable. Families are not formed and sustained in the ways we are used to. The rigor with which business leaders have to think about managing their companies in the face of tough global competition has changed the way the public views school management. Yet schools themselves are often very conservative with regard to change, and their resistance to change is legend. In the midst of all this change, we ask our school administrators to chart a way through the forest and lead us in it. It is no small challenge.

As Dr. Bill Holland points out so well in this book, the cost of the failure of school leaders is enormous, both to individuals and to communities. When a principal or superintendent fails, the failure is felt throughout the community, as a disruption of the lives of city or town officials, school board members, teachers, families, and most of all, students. The recriminations, hard feelings, and bitterness that often flow from this kind of conflict can be felt for a generation or more. And the real-dollar costs of those now-defunct initiatives begun by the failed leader are often very high and can ripple through the system for years. As those of us who have lived through such public debacles know so well, it's not pretty.

Through three all-too-real case studies, Dr. Holland helps us to understand that, in this time of unprecedented change, of all the virtues we look for in our leaders, the most important is flexibility, the ability to be the willow that bends in a storm, not the oak that breaks. That kind of leadership involves the ability to suspend immediate judgment, to seek good counsel, to understand that the past lives on in schools, and to acknowledge that wisdom does not reside only in the corner office. It involves seeking out and then building on the aspirations of a community, empowering teachers and students to live and work in the light of a compelling, shared vision.

Finally, Dr. Holland draws on his many years of experience as a teacher, principal, superintendent, and professor to give us a wonderful series of tips on how to select the kind of leaders we need in this era. His ideas are both profound and practical, balancing our high expectations with the real-life dynamics of schools, school board, and teachers. Rather than charging out in pursuit of candidates who have succeeded elsewhere, for example, we would be well served by using the search and selection process to help affirm our values and needs, taking up the hunt only when we have agreed just what the game is. Making a commitment to spend this time at the beginning of the search process can reduce the rate of failure in the end. Selecting and supporting successful school leaders is what this book is all about. Nothing is more important.

Robert L. Carothers
President, University of Rhode Island
Kingston, Rhode Island

Introduction

Becky was a bright and capable honors student with a newly minted master's degree in school leadership who lasted only six months after assuming a principalship in a small suburban elementary school. A leader in her graduate cohort and an experienced teacher in a number of school settings, she had completed a full semester as an intern in another district, where mentor, teachers, students, and parents raved about her performance. Less than a year later, Becky was involved in a contentious and litigious termination process with her school district. What went wrong? Was she doomed to failure before she started?

Hired as a new elementary principal from a neighboring school district, Ruth came highly recommended. She had transformed her previous school by developing and implementing a new reading system that produced significant results in student achievement. Unfortunately, Ruth immediately found herself in trouble with her teachers, who asked the superintendent to take immediate action to quell the growing unrest. The principal–staff conflict became so intense that several of the teachers took extended sick leave due to stress. Eventually, Ruth received a settlement when forced to resign. What led to this disaster?

Judd was an experienced superintendent hired in a medium-size school district following twenty-one years of much-lauded success in three other districts. Following a very publicized superior board evaluation after his first year, he abruptly resigned under board pressure and received a contract buy-out in his second year. What went wrong so quickly?

The three cases are taken from real situations with the identities of people and places changed. They are meant to assist aspiring school leaders as they venture into today's schools and how they operate. Graduate programs that prepare school leaders can teach all the leadership courses they want, but the individual fit of a "leadership personality" with the diverse cultures of America's schools is difficult to predict. Well-supervised internships are helpful in providing aspiring principals with valuable insights; however, internships are limited in fully preparing prospective principals for the unique challenges awaiting them when they assume the mantle of principal or superintendent of schools.

This book also goes further than just looking at novice school leaders who make beginning mistakes. Two of the cases presented involve experienced school leaders who leave successful situations and are recruited into new positions. In such cases, selection committees (sometimes at considerable expense) go through elaborate public processes to get the right person for their leadership vacancy. Too often, after disaster occurs, a simplistic explanation, such as "it was a bad match," is offered as an excuse. The real question, however, still remains: "How could seasoned school leaders and the good people who serve on selection committees make such monumental and costly mistakes?"

I candidly admit that after twenty-six years as a superintendent, school-level administrator, and teacher, and seventeen years as a professor of educational leadership involved in training principals and superintendents, answers to this question still evade me. Shockingly, "can't miss" school leaders still end up failing.

The social and emotional characteristics of leaders are definitely playing a larger role in determining the success of today's school leaders. New expectations for improved student achievement results and the accompanying state and federal standards assessment and accountability systems are calling for more knowledgeable and competent instructional leaders who have well-honed interpersonal skills. The accelerating forces of change are requiring new school leaders to build collaborative relationships with teachers with the common goal being improved achievement for all children. Without the human relations skills needed to gain the respect, credibility, and trust of teachers, students, and the greater community, new school leaders will not succeed.

The three case studies presented in Chapters 5, 6, and 7 illustrate the increased stress, responsibilities, and demands placed upon contemporary school leaders and how the personal and human dimensions of leadership are increasingly more important than ever before in managing change and establishing trusting relationships between school leaders and teachers.

The cases tell of the physical and mental anguish experienced by the three school leaders when facing the loss of their jobs and their reputations. Under intense public scrutiny, their careers and futures as professional educators are at stake. How can these tragedies be avoided?

The last chapter calls attention to what can be done to improve the quality of candidate selection decisions and how to avoid the number of personnel calamities and the aftermath explosions that many times occur when poor school leader selections are made. Some helpful advice on steps to be considered by selection committees and other officials in making those key leadership decisions, which are crucial to the success of today's schools, can also be found in the last chapter.

1

What Is Leadership? It Depends on Whom You Ask

Ah, the age-old question. What is leadership? Although I crafted my own operational definition of leadership many years ago, the actual teaching of leadership to aspiring school leaders is another matter. The problem is that leadership means different things to different people. Also, when you ask people to give you their definition of leadership, you realize they don't have one, or they assume everyone knows what it is, so why define it?

It is amusing to listen to people who believe they know what leadership is explaining why their boss got fired. "He isn't a good leader" is a common response. A host of reasons why the boss failed then follows, generally describing a list of the boss's personality flaws that resulted in his demise.

My definition of leadership is constructed from my years of experience as an educational leader. I favor situational leadership theory combined with a leader's capacity to modify her style when needed. Such a definition puts a heavy emphasis on a leader having a solid repertoire of group and interpersonal skills in order to successfully share her vision and core values with those she leads. Consequently, relational skills are given a high ranking on my leadership scale when it comes to training aspiring school leaders, assuming, of course, that the prerequisite intelligence, communication skills, and knowledge base are also present.

I must confess that after teaching leadership courses for nearly twenty years to aspiring school principals and other school leaders, I still wonder if the concept of leadership can ever really be taught. Has all this effort been in vain? Has it made any difference in the working lives of those past students who ventured into the dark jungle as leaders of contemporary school organizations?

Oh yes, I tried some creative approaches in applying leadership theory to practice. For example, when using the case study method, class discussions were lively, entertaining, and provocative. Embellishing the discussions with tales from my twenty-six years as a practicing school administrator added needed spice to the instruction.

But did these intended learning experiences have any real effect on the future leadership behavior of a new generation of school leaders who interacted with me for a semester or two in a graduate classroom or in a one-day workshop? Put more succinctly, can leadership truly be taught to adults who have already established patterns of social interaction skills? Are some behavior patterns simply in the bones and unchangeable? Should we put greater credence into the saying, "Leaders are born and not made" than we do?

Do we utilize what research teaches us about personality types when we select school leaders and place them in contexts where it is imperative they possess certain high-level interpersonal skills if they are to succeed? And finally, are we going about the business of preparing school leaders in college graduate programs in the right way? These questions need to be more fully addressed.

The fine work of Daniel Goleman, Michael Fullan, and Robert Greenleaf makes even me wonder if following the advice of these noted theorists really can cause a change in leadership behavior for everyone. Some people are capable of interpersonal changes and others are not. Unfortunately, many school leaders have rooted and ingrained behaviors that are a result of years of conditioning; change for these leaders is difficult, if not impossible.

Goleman's research on emotional intelligence[1] provides fertile ground to understand the importance and relationship of well-honed group and individual interpersonal skills to successful leadership. Leaders who are self-aware, self-regulated, motivated, empathetic, and have social skill proficiency have the tools to be successful leaders. A school leader who rates high in all five categories apparently will be a successful leader.

Unfortunately, it might be impossible with the life experience that has already shaped a new principal's personality to adapt accordingly and rank high on Goleman's emotional intelligence list. For example, a school context might call for a high level of empathy from its leader. One might be capable of learning how to be more understanding and skillful in treating people according to their emotional reactions, but how do they learn this? How and when do you find out that a particular leadership need or leadership style is crucial to your success before you sign on as the new principal? How does a search committee really learn that a prospective new principal suffers from poor self-awareness? The width of the gap between a person's self perception and the general perception of others is also difficult to identify through reference checks and interviews.

From his futurist perch, Fullan[2] contends that at a time when principal leadership needs to be more proactive, principals find themselves in a least favorable position to provide it. He sees principals overloaded with a host of disjointed demands fostering what he terms, "contextual dependency." He calls for principals to "think out of the box" by respecting those they want to silence, moving toward the danger of forming new alliances, managing emotionally as well as rationally, and fighting for lost causes. He stipulates that leaders have to craft their own theories of change, consistently testing them against new situations.

Fullan admits that there are no packaged solutions to successfully leading school organizations. Fullan's advice reminds me of the old definition of leadership that states, "A leader is someone who can successfully play a variety of roles well." Fullan doesn't tell principals how to foster more collaborative work cultures (the goal, of course, being increased student achievement) but instead urges them to courageously follow the complex road of change by gathering the needed insights, data, and direction working with the organization's unique personalities and cultural conditions.

This is all fine; however, it assumes that the leader possesses or has the capacity to acquire enough of Goleman's five dimensions of emotional intelligence to have the adaptability and interpersonal skill to navigate the cultural waters.

Finally, there is the work of Robert Greenleaf,[3] an executive with IBM, who developed a concept called "servant leadership" over twenty years ago. He asserts that with servant leadership the power to lead is symbiotic, that it derives from followers who are freed from fear and self-doubt by the leader who validates them. Thus, he postulates that those he would lead must create the necessary environment for a leader to take bold action. Making followers more competent and more confident thus becomes the fundamental work of a servant leader.

For example, a college president acquaintance of mine feels that aggressive listening is the key act to validating people and admitted that although he holds a set of core beliefs, he is still open to new ideas and new possibilities.[4] At the same time, he does not shy away from controversy and feels he has made the hard decisions when public scrutiny has been intense.

Following Fullan's suggestion, he crafts his own change agenda by combining his belief in servant leadership with a passionate concern for creating a culture that reflects quality. Interestingly, he follows a path set by Deming[5] and others with the goal being the creation of a work culture where individuals feel more empowered to act on their own initiative to improve their work and the work of others.

Is this a perfect leadership system to which everyone has bought in? No, it isn't, because leaders are human and the organizations they lead are dynamic, changing, complex, diverse, and many times absolutely mystifying. At times, do the president's voids and quirks in certain leadership areas run counter to his espoused leadership philosophy? Of course, they do.

However, because of his high level of self-awareness, his adaptability, and his personal integrity he has had a successful tenure and a list of notable achievements at his university over the course of fifteen years.

He does admit that, although difficult, he has gradually changed his leadership style and behaviors over the years in order to address new contextual variables that have emerged. He clearly feels this capacity to change has greatly contributed to his success.

SUMMARY

Leadership is a complex concept, and difficult to define. Aspiring and experienced principals and superintendents must possess a high level of self-awareness regarding their strengths and weaknesses in motivating people to pursue common goals. The ability to adapt to changing conditions in the environment in which they work is also crucial to their success.

Effective leadership depends on the leader possessing a range of interpersonal skills, but because of past conditioning some leaders might be incapable of developing new behavioral skills. A leader that realizes his limitations will carefully determine the context where his leadership personality and style will best fit and where his chance for success is most likely.

Finally, leaders need followers. Leaders must realize that failure to empower people will limit their success in an organization. A leader who is not willing to share some of her power greatly reduces her chance for success.

2

Adapting to or Changing the Organizational Culture: It's Not Easy

In recent years, the leadership challenges presented by the school and school district environment have received increased attention by educational writers.[6] School leaders are asked to change the organizational culture of schools[7] that are beset by obstacles to school improvement.

School leaders are directed to be social engineers in order to change the staid thinking that block schools from becoming more student-centered and achievement-oriented. They are asked to become visionary leaders, creating communities of learners where collaboration and shared decision-making are the norm.[8] They must create and maintain a healthy and open organizational climate in schools, where the opinions and participation of students, teachers, parents, and community members are valued.

It is understandable why many school leaders find their jobs difficult, if not impossible. If they are not placed in a situation where their leadership is accepted and respected, they are headed for failure. If they find themselves in what might be considered an impossible situation for them or the wrong situation or match for their leadership style, they have no choice but to contemplate leaving.

Even with honorable intentions, great ideas, and a passion for change, principal frustration and failure lurk if school leaders are powerless and the organizational culture to effect positive change is absent.

6

In numerous instances, school leaders who are well respected and liked suddenly resign for no apparent reason. When you search further, you learn that such leaders have reached a peak in their frustration level and seek other situations where they can better employ their energy and skills and achieve more rewarding results.

Following the example of the college president mentioned earlier, in order for school leaders to achieve success and not fail, it could mean modifying their leadership style and behaviors. It might also mean drawing upon a hidden reserve of patience or employing newly learned relationship skills and behaviors. The key issue concerns the leader's openness, willingness, and capacity to change or, better stated, "recraft" their leadership.

Unfortunately, school leaders entering a new situation might not have the luxury of time to adjust and adapt accordingly after some beginning conflicts or misreads on their part. Initially, everyone is watching and there is little margin for error or costly mistakes. This, of course, depends upon the severity of the conflict and the controversy it generates.

In other situations, school leaders are asked to sacrifice some of their long-held values and beliefs. Head-on collisions occur, caused by differences in philosophy or experience between new school leaders and their staff. When placed in such situations, leaders are forced to remain firm in their positions or lose credibility.

Receiving support from parents and key school officials is also important, as the political influence, power, and opposition of teacher unions frequently weaken the needed support from the superintendent and school board. This corroding support generally obscures the facts and the local media then portrays the school leader poorly. Weathering this type of conflict is often beyond the control or capacity of the school leader, forcing the leader to fight on matter of principle or to step sideways until another time.

SUMMARY

The burning questions still persist. How do you prepare future school leaders to cope with the magnitude of the different leadership challenges presented in today's schools? How do you point them in the right direction and provide them with the proper training to be successful in a variety of diverse school cultures? Can it be done better than we are currently doing it in our educational leadership programs? Yes, it can be done better, but it's not easy.

3

Teaching Leadership

My brief review of the literature illustrates the complexity and elusiveness of trying to define, as well as teach, leadership and leadership theory. Nevertheless, as a professor of educational leadership, I charged ahead year after year introducing a lexicon of leadership theory generated by four decades of educational writers.

I inundated my students with theoretical constructs ranging from the trait theory of leadership, to management by objectives, to collaborative leadership. I didn't forget system theory, transactional and transformational leadership, shared leadership, facilitative leadership, situational leadership, reflective practice, total quality management, servant leadership, moral leadership, and many others.

I urged students to use these constructs as lenses to critically observe the leadership styles of school leaders they shadowed and the principal mentors who supervised their internships. The hope was that by some internal transference process, direct observation of school leaders and on-the-job training would allow these budding administrators to closely examine and better understand their own leadership strengths and weaknesses.

By exposing students to successful mentors and providing them with the latest and popular leadership theory and practice, successful assimilation of knowledge would occur, allowing them to successfully hone their leadership skills and abilities.

Unfortunately, in spite of my efforts, several outstanding students who were appointed to educational leadership positions failed miserably. The short answers to these tragedies usually were: "It was a bad fit," "The new principal didn't understand the culture of the school," "Colleges are not properly preparing these people for the reality of today's schools," "The personality of this individual quickly alienated her subordinates," "The emotional instability of the man when faced with a major challenge lead to his demise," or "We need to attract a better quality applicant pool in the future."

What follows are three actual cases of failed leadership. What led to the series of bad choices made by school leaders and search committees? Are the school leaders solely to blame for these tragedies? What type of leader might have achieved success in each scenario? These are but a few of the questions raised.

4

Background of the Cases

The three cases selected for this book describe the experiences of two principals and one superintendent in two different states. Although written from notes gathered from real situations, names and places have been changed. Some embellishments have also been added to underscore several key points. Some of the data comes from interviews with key participants while other data is generated from the actual direct experience of the writer. The accounts are not meant to be factual; however, the sequence and nature of events closely mirror what actually happened.

In all three cases, the school leaders had achieved considerable success up to this point in their careers. The principal in the first case was a veteran teacher and one of the top students in her graduate program. She had just finished a principal internship where she received strong recommendations from her mentor and faculty members. Interestingly, she was offered an assistant principal position at the elementary school where she interned, but instead chose to accept an eighteen-month contract with more money and prestige as principal of a small elementary school in her hometown.

The principal in the second case was hired from a neighboring district where her success and reputation for high standards were well known. She was only offered a one-year contract. The school board had had a bad experience with the last principal who had been given a three-year contract. As a result, they adopted a new policy limiting the next principal's contract to one year.

The third case describes a well-respected superintendent who had an exceptional 16-year record of success as a superintendent in two other school districts. He was completing his second year of a three-year contract in a new community.

In every case, a thorough search was conducted that included a series of interviews with search committees, superintendents, and school board members. Members of the search committees took on-site visits to the superintendent's school district and to the experienced principal's elementary school. Public forums for teachers, parents, and community members were conducted allowing feedback from all interested parties. Written recommendations were sought, received, and reviewed.

The superintendent and school board members conducted telephone reference checks (it should be noted that search consultants were not used in the recruiting of any of the three school leaders). During the interviews, core questions were asked and scored for all candidates interviewed. The finalists were given an opportunity to tour the schools and talk with faculty, students, and parents. Excitement ran high. Enthusiasm and satisfaction occurred when the first choice in each of the three searches accepted a contract. What could go wrong? The most highly qualified candidates had been hired.

5

Me Against Them: The Case of Becky Hazard, Promising First-Year Principal

"Settlement Lets Former Principal Resign"

The newspaper article cryptically stated that the eight-month legal battle between principal Becky Hazard and the Pleasantville School Board had finally come to an end. It read: "Southside Elementary School Principal Becky Hazard and the School Board have agreed to the terms of her departure from the school district. The settlement will allow for Hazard to resign from her contract on June 30, and rescinds the school board's January vote to fire her, according to a joint release announced last night."

The article said that the agreement ended a legal battle that had proceeded to both the state superior and supreme courts, where all litigation would now be dismissed without prejudice.

The school department agreed to give Hazard a financial settlement of $30,000 and admitted that it spent over $50,000 on litigation. Becky was to be paid her full salary and benefits for the year and receive a letter of recommendation from the superintendent. In actuality, the total district cost was closer to $200,000 by the time you factored in the cost of Becky's full salary and benefits and the per diem cost for her replacement.

The human cost was also apparent. In addition to $35,000 in out-of-pocket legal expenses, Becky had medical costs for counseling and treatment of family members and for her own hospitalization for mental stress. The public embarrassment and the damage of reputations to the parties involved were also apparent as the bitter dispute raged for months like an unchecked wildfire in state and local newspapers.

BECKY AND SOUTHSIDE

The problem started immediately after Becky's appointment as the new principal of the Southside Elementary School. Southside was situated in a residential seaside village in the town of Pleasantville that had a year-round population of approximately 30,000. It drew students primarily from professional, middle-class parents who had watched the value of their homes escalate in recent years. Some summer homes were rented during the school year, resulting in a small transient student population. The school served approximately 340 students with a professional staff of thirty-eight. Although it was still a high-achieving school, where students performed well on state assessment tests, scores had been gradually declining during the past five years.

Starting her job at mid-year, Becky was genuinely excited to lead a school that had experienced considerable instability in the past five years. Southside had had six principals in those five years, including four interim principals restricted by state law to seventy-five day contracts; one principal who died on the job; and the last principal who resigned at mid-year. One teacher characterized the last principal as someone who lacked respect from the staff because they "never took to his style." She claimed that staff morale had sunk to a new low. She also freely admitted that because of the long void in stable and effective leadership, the faculty enjoyed "running the show" and, in fact, resisted authority when asked to change direction and routine—especially when that direction came from temporary or incompetent principals.

At first blush, Southside appeared to be an impossible situation for a first-year principal. The truth was that neither Becky nor the search committee, for that matter, considered her a neophyte administrator. A spirited and enthusiastic woman in her early 40s with three school-age children, she and her family had recently moved to Pleasantville. She had more than twenty years experience in education, having taught in high school and in elementary school. She held a master's degree in both teaching and administration and had worked as a trainer and supervisor in an educational publishing firm. As previously mentioned, her principal internship was a rousing success. Highly knowledgeable, well read, and articulate about curriculum and instruction, she had confidence, inner strength, and energy about her.

Some members of the search committee worried about Becky's imposing and emphatic personality. This concern resulted in the committee taking an extraordinarily long time to make a recommendation. The dissenters eventually acquiesced to the majority, who felt that Becky's professional and personal maturity, confidence, and intelligence were exactly what were needed to turn Southside around.

One teacher provided some interesting insight. She explained, "Teachers were apprehensive and cautious when Mrs. Hazard first arrived. Everyone tried to give her the benefit of the doubt, but we were leery because the previous principal had burned us. It was difficult to trust administrators in our school district because so many came and went. We had a lack of communication between all levels of administration and staff and not just in our school. We were seldom asked for our input. It was an us-against-them atmosphere that led to mistrust and failure."

OPPOSITION FORMS

Becky's "benefit of the doubt" lasted about two weeks. Although most teachers appeared friendly, several seemed to ignore her, especially the strong union types. They definitely were an independent group, wanting to be left alone in their classrooms.

She decided to assert herself and make her presence known. She refused to be what she termed, a "figurehead" principal. How could she be if she were to take up the charge given her by the superintendent and "reclaim the school for the children"?

When she asked for teacher input on an upcoming open house, no input was given. This surprised her. Do they expect her to do all the work? When she tried to form a committee to look at a key issue, the union teacher leaders quickly advised her, "Things are not done that way here."

Becky also met opposition from her own secretary, whom she observed acted more like an assistant principal than a school secretary. After several instances of disloyalty and verbal reprimands, Becky observed the secretary rummaging through some personal items in her desk. When she gave her a letter of reprimand, her secretary filed a union grievance. Teachers supported the secretary who had worked at the school for a number of years.

She also observed some teachers doing some inappropriate things in violation of policy and good sense. She saw two teachers treating children in ways she could not tolerate and felt compelled to question their practices and seek correction. Word spreads quickly among the faculty that the principal was on the prowl.

Obviously, Becky was very shaken by her initial reception at Southside. She privately confided to a friend, "How can I be a moral leader in such an immoral place?"

One teacher offered another explanation, "Mrs. Hazard came in with a very strong take-charge attitude. This did not go over well with the staff. She was definitely the type of administrator that liked to make unilateral decisions. Whenever questioned about decisions, her response was that it was her decision and not ours—even if it had a direct impact on our classroom."

"For example, she made several decisions that negatively affected the school climate, such as listening to parent complaints and then acting on them without consulting the teachers involved. She created new policies without researching past practices and current practices. She made many decisions without much forethought. In my opinion, Mrs. Hazard's personality was not one that worked with this staff."

The incident that best illustrates the philosophical differences and growing rift between Becky and her faculty was the "crème pie affair." Becky and parent association members organized a fundraiser that involved, among other things, students throwing whipped crème pies in the face of the principal and other staff volunteers. Two union leaders approached Becky shortly after learning of the pie activity, and in what she felt was a threatening manner, informed her she couldn't do such a thing because it promoted violence and was a waste of food. As a result, teachers did not participate in the activity.

The local newspapers seized the opportunity to sensationalize the crème pie conflict between Becky and her teachers. Eventually, the school superintendent agreed to attend the fundraiser and have his face smothered with pie. According to Becky, this represented the last time the superintendent came to her defense.

SUPERINTENDENT INTERVENTION

Henry Lowe, the school superintendent, realized that he had to intervene at Southside and stem the brooding tide of a situation that might get out of control. Because of the immediate negative reaction to Becky's leadership, he met with her and attempted to counsel her. His impression was that Becky was somewhat opinionated and defensive when he offered constructive criticism. (It should be noted that Lowe was only in his second year as Pleasantville superintendent and his leadership was being watched closely by the teachers' union, parents, and school board members.)

Lowe was also faced with a growing budget deficit, an incredible recent turnover of school administrators throughout the district, and a powerful, active, and confrontational teachers' union. In hindsight, he readily confessed that Southside was a microcosm of the Pleasantville school district. "For administrators to survive, they had better not be mediocre. In Pleasantville, you will get knocked down if you are not an exceptional school leader." He explained that teacher union leaders were very skillful in pushing people to one position against a principal.

Becky faulted Lowe for not providing her with clear performance goals and refusing her initial request for a mentor. Because of what he observed as a lethal powder keg at Southside, Lowe decided that it was necessary for him to assume the responsibility of mentoring Becky.

UNION UPSET

In spite of Lowe's mentoring, the situation at Southside worsened. The union reported a number of alleged incidents of Becky's poor leadership to Lowe.

One teacher summarized several incidences, "Mrs. Hazard gave teachers and parents different answers to the same question. She made mistakes, like locking herself in her dark office and refusing to come out during our open house when a student was injured. She allowed a child to be picked up at school by someone not authorized to do so. The other day, she swore at a teacher during an argument in the library."

Becky strongly refuted these allegations and offered detailed explanations to Lowe. She contended that a few malcontents set her up and distorted the incidents.

Unfortunately, formal grievances from Southside union representatives continued to flood Lowe's office. Lowe talked individually with several teachers to gather staff reactions. He called a meeting between him, the union leadership, and Becky. His purpose was to forge a written understanding as a means to get Becky and the union working together.

Becky was perplexed with Lowe's tactics and questioned its appropriateness, because he was asking the union president to approve an agreement that included a plan of improvement for her. Nevertheless, Becky signed the agreement in an attempt to end the hostility at the school.

Meanwhile, several teachers were angered at Lowe's apparent initial support for Becky and what they felt was a lack of teacher support. One frustrated teacher cried, "Lowe believes her over an entire staff that have documented incidents that the school is out of control. She is causing personal safety issues here that can't be ignored. The union has filed many grievances, but in the end it is only when the pot boils over that something will be done."

The pot did boil over when school resumed the following fall. Grievances continued to multiply and Becky began to receive nasty, unsigned letters. Union representatives refused to talk to her. Although there were a few teachers who quietly came to her defense, the majority succumbed to the gang mentality that spread throughout the school.

LOWE'S HOT SEAT

By the end of the first month of school, Lowe painfully realized that reaching a peace accord between Becky and her faculty was close to impossible. The situation was unraveling. Relationships continued to deteriorate. He was receiving intense pressure from teachers to take some action.

Parents were voicing concerns. Influenced by teacher feedback, some parents viewed Becky as the major culprit, while others quietly admired her spunk. Generally, parents were not taking sides in the dispute, but instead were expressing deep concerns for their children because of the growing chaos in the school. Some complaints were being directly registered with school board members. Lowe was truly on the hot seat. The situation was reaching a crisis point.

At the same time, Lowe's feelings about Becky's complicity in the problem were also shifting. Based on teacher feedback and his own impressions gathered from interactions with Becky, he was now convinced that Becky didn't have the emotional stability to be an effective principal at Southside or, for that matter, to even survive the school year. Bold action on his part was needed.

Lowe acted. In late September, he placed Becky on an involuntary leave of absence. Two weeks later, meeting with the school board in executive session, he received approval to offer Becky an assistant principal position in a larger elementary school across town. After notification of this proposed transfer and apparent demotion, Becky immediately hired a lawyer.

ACCEPT OR FIGHT?

When lawyers enter a dispute between the school board and one of its employees, the conflict is guaranteed to become more complex, lengthier, more intense, more hostile, and of course, more expensive. Such was the case in the legal battle between Becky and the Pleasantville superintendent and school board.

Prior to meeting with her new lawyer, Becky was faced with an agonizing decision. Should she accept the assistant principal transfer or refuse the offer and fight to keep her job at Southside?

She sought advice from friends, relatives, and from her college mentor, Professor Hathaway. Hathaway told her to accept the lesser job, cut her losses, and escape further damage to her reputation. He argued that her best bet was to finish the school year in splendid fashion as an assistant principal and put Southside behind her. Rational people would understand.

One of Becky's friends put it best, "God Almighty couldn't turn that school around given its past history and culture. Get out while you can."

Professor Hathaway had even more advice. "Becky, there are no winners in a battle like yours. You are putting your future career as a school leader in jeopardy. Things will only get increasingly painful for you and your family as charges and counter charges from both sides litter the local and state newspapers. Are you prepared to handle the personal anguish?"

Outwardly, Becky agreed with Hathaway's advice; however, burning inside was a feeling of personal unfairness and mistreatment and a strong desire to let the public know the real truth at Southside. She told Hathaway, "I plan to follow the advice of my lawyer."

Hal Bickford, Becky's lawyer, convinced her to refuse the assistant principal position and not to report to work after her leave expired. Bickford contended that Becky had been denied her civil rights because Lowe and the school board had privately discussed her job performance in executive session. He opined that the state's open meeting law had not been followed and Becky's due process rights were thereby violated.

With Becky's refusal to report to work, Lowe was forced to respond to questions from the local media. He was quoted as saying, "Becky Smith's failure to report to work makes her absent without leave and the matter will soon be brought to the school board." He also attempted to ease the minds of parents by writing them a personal letter informing them that all Southside students "had been and still were safe and secure in their school."

At the end of October, Lowe sent Becky a letter informing her that he would recommend to the school board in a future meeting that she be fired for failure to report to work. That meeting was never held.

LITIGATION BEGINS

Hal Bickford went to work. He filed a petition with superior court to stop the school board from conducting a termination meeting. The superior court judge got the two parties together to agree that nothing would be done before he had a chance to conduct a formal hearing in two weeks.

At the preliminary hearing, Becky discovered some shocking and upsetting information. In an affidavit filed by the school board attorney, Lowe stated that Becky was being investigated for misconduct and was removed from Southside because he "feared for the safety of the children." No one had told Becky that she was being investigated for misconduct. She vehemently called the charges, "absolutely ridiculous."

Broached by two reporters, Becky responded to the charges in the affidavit. Becky later admitted that she made some comments that got twisted by the reporters. Upon reading the articles, Becky was so disturbed she wailed, "I want to die. Why did I wake up this morning?"

Becky now directed her wrath at Lowe. She was convinced it was more than a case of his capitulating to the union leadership; he was now telling lies.

A TWISTING ROAD

A few weeks later, the superior court judge heard the case and shortly thereafter issued a preliminary injunction against Lowe, the school board, and the town of Pleasantville.

He found that the school board had not met its burden of proof and that Becky had met her burden of proof in establishing that there had been a violation of the open meeting law. He thus declared the adverse actions taken against Becky during the board's closed session, "null and void pending trial." In addition, the judge added, "Mrs. Hazard's reputation appears harmed, her ability to continue on her career path in school administration is tarnished, simply because the school board was quick at the draw. The logical solution for an improper dismissal is reinstatement. The court is also not convinced of any danger to students."

Becky felt vindicated and looked forward to returning to Southside, although clearly with much trepidation. Lowe immediately met with the Southside faculty and informed them that no matter what he had to do he would make sure Becky didn't step foot on school property.

Becky's sense of elation did not last long, nor did she ever return to Southside. The school board appealed the superior court decision to the state supreme court. The board's position was one of admitting that they had made a mistake in violating the open meetings law; however, they asserted that the judge's decision did not deny them the opportunity to convene another hearing with Becky and her lawyer regarding her job performance.

Based on their redoing of a wrong, the board argued they have the right to convene a hearing and vote to terminate Becky if they had cause. She, in turn, had the right to a public hearing to appeal any adverse vote taken. They further argued that the superior court decision reinstating Becky should not remain as a permanent solution blocking them from removing her as principal if they found cause.

The state supreme court agreed with the school board's position, thereby allowing them to proceed with a termination hearing. During the trial, the press received a copy of transcript that Becky's lawyer had filed with the court responding to some of the charges against her. In the transcript, Lowe and the school board lawyer described Becky's conduct as principal as "dangerous."

When hearing that she was being described as dangerous, Becky was devastated. She e-mailed a friend, "After today's article, I will probably never work again. I have been slandered beyond any hope of repair. They are ruining my life with all these lies. Is there a witness relocation program for ruined ex-principals? My only respite at this point is to cry."

TERMINATION HEARING

Before it acted on a vote to fire Becky and deny renewal of her contract at the end of the school year, Hal Bickford requested a closed meeting with the superintendent and school board. He reasoned that if a vote to terminate took place, they would get an opportunity to appeal and a full public hearing would be held where he and Becky intended to "come out with guns blazing."

Prior to this closed session, one hundred Southside parents and teachers convened in order to voice their opinions and concerns. Emotions were running high. Becky observed union representatives writing down the names of parents who spoke in support of her. She turned to her lawyer explaining it was just another case of intimidation by the union leadership.

After a two-hour closed session with Becky and Bickford, the school board came out of executive session at 11 p.m. to publicly vote on Becky's future. About thirty-five people remained to hear the results.

The vote was 6 to 1 in support of Lowe's recommendation to terminate Becky.

School board members explained their vote to those people who waited patiently throughout the night for a decision.

"One thing I have heard as the people spoke was the frustration of not knowing, not having the facts. Just through the process of listening to Dr. Lowe describe the results of his investigation and the advice of Mrs. Hazard's counsel not to have her respond during our meeting, with the information before me, I support the motion," said one board member.

Another offered, "For $85,585, I expect excellence, not immaturity, or impatience, or outbursts of anger. I support the motion."

The chairwoman of the board had two reasons for supporting termination. "It was not just one issue, there were many over a period of many, many months and not a lot of improvement," she said. "There were many supports in place, but no change. The children deserve a top-notch administrator."

The one board dissenter indicated that he went to the hearing with a few questions, and the answers persuaded him to vote no. "The first thing the superintendent said was each and any incident by itself would not be sufficient to bring us to this point."

He continued, "I feel Mrs. Hazard went into an environment where they were looking for her mistakes. It's not an environment an administrator should work in and I cannot support paying two principals' salaries."

DENOUEMENT

The public appeal hearing where the "facts" could be heard by the citizens of Pleasantville never came to past. As so often happens, both sides met after the termination action and the lawyers worked out a settlement in order to stop the bloodletting and the spiraling litigation costs.

The settlement gave each side an opportunity to "save face" and avoid ugly public confrontations where the press could have a feeding frenzy.

Becky admitted that there would always be a part of her that wishes that the truth had surfaced. However, her health and her family had suffered enough. Shortly after the hearing, Becky was hospitalized with mental stress but recovered nicely and got on with her life.

Her professional reputation, however, was tarnished. She submitted multiple applications to other school districts, attempting to find another job as principal or assistant principal. She had difficulty getting interviews. No one seemed to want her. She felt like damaged goods. Two principal jobs where she was granted preliminary interviews were unsuccessful ventures—especially as she tried to explain what had happened to her in Pleasantville.

Becky eventually accepted an educational administrative position outside of public education. In a few years, when memories fade, she hopes to return to public education.

CASE ANALYSIS

Hindsight is always helpful in analyzing human behavior and the mistakes people make. Upon reflection, Becky now admits that if she had it to do over again, she would accept Lowe's offer to transfer to the assistant principal's position.

At the time of the offer, her relationship with Lowe was at a healthy point and early enough for her to overcome fallout from the Southside debacle. She had no idea how hurtful the eventual struggle would be for both she and her family and how damaging it would be to her professional reputation.

Although a veteran teacher, verbally gifted, and highly intelligent, Becky was politically naïve. She stepped directly into a firestorm and was not prepared to cope with the challenges presented by a powerful teachers' union and a politically astute superintendent that many claim ran for cover when Becky's ship was sinking. Lowe, in particular, had the political savvy not to take on the union at this time of his young tenure. He frankly admitted, "Becky took on the wrong union, in the wrong state, at the wrong time."

Becky obviously made some beginning mistakes from which she

never recovered. She provided one telling illustration. Apparently in her first few months, she decided to take the student-placement assignment responsibility for the next school year away from the teachers who had been doing it for a number of years. She underestimated how disturbing such a decision would be for a faculty that for years had assumed this responsibility. In hindsight, she now feels she should have backed off on that change for a year or two.

Her take-charge attitude also contributed to her problems. Rather than assuming an authority-type posture, she should have worked on building a degree of initial trust, respect, and acceptance by her staff. She should have temporarily postponed her change agenda and focused instead on utilizing those leadership behaviors that improve rather than exacerbate principal–faculty relations.

Becky pushed too hard, too soon. A softer, more humble approach was needed, but her passion to change the Southside culture stopped her from adopting this approach.

Her emotional make-up was also in conflict with the culture at Southside. When confronted, her first reaction was one of anger and to strike back by asserting her authority. Instead, she needed to find areas where she could interest staff in working collaboratively with her, areas where they would have meaningful influence in making change. In year one, she needed to let the staff establish the change agenda and then work beside them and build a series of small successes together. Unfortunately, her ego needs and reluctance of teachers to participate prevented this approach from happening.

Search committee members who had had reservations about Becky's strong personality were right. The majority of the committee, as well as Lowe and the school board, misread the type of leadership needed at Southside and, in the process, contributed to the misery that followed for Becky, her staff, and school officials.

If mentoring were ever needed for a beginning principal, Becky needed a respected mentor (who was not in the chain of command) from day one. This need should have been clearly apparent to the search committee, Lowe, and the school board. Some of the money later wasted on litigation would have been better used to provide Becky desperately needed outside counsel and assistance. Would Becky have survived? We will never know.

Becky's pride also played a key role in her decision to take on the teachers' union, the superintendent, and the school board. Pride and obviously heightened insecurity might have gotten in the way during her meetings with Lowe when he perceived her as being defensive and opinionated.

Becky also believed that the superintendent and school board covered up the true problems at Southside. She reeled at being blamed for problems that she felt were created more by years of administrative benign neglect at Southside than by her lack of leadership.

In her decision to fight, she took up the cause at great personal sacrifice. It took considerable courage for a novice principal to overcome the insurmountable odds she faced. However, she went forward with token, silent support from parents and a few teachers trying to improve a school situation for children and their parents.

Unfortunately, Becky did not win the battle. She, Lowe, and the school board were all losers. In the process, Becky paid a high price emotionally. In the final settlement between herself and the school board, it was agreed that there would be no public disclosure of records of the trial or hearings. No personal statements by either party were to be made to the press other than the joint statement announcing the settlement. Becky's wish for the whole truth to be known by the general public would never be realized.

6

The Hammer or the Velvet Glove? The Case of Ruth Maloney, Highly Regarded Principal

THE BRIGGS SISTERS

It was a bleak and dreary November afternoon as superintendent of schools, Steven Knowles, glanced out his office window at the impressive oak tree with its bare-boned branches stripped of the last remnants of the brilliant New England fall foliage of only a few weeks ago.

In his second year as superintendent in Tilton, a small, wealthy suburb of 18,000 people located inside the sprawling interstates that encircle Boston, Knowles looks at his calendar to see who was next on his schedule.

At that moment, his secretary knocked on his door and announced that Lucy and Ethel Briggs, long-time teachers at the Wales Elementary School, were present for their four o'clock meeting. Knowles had no idea what the sisters wanted but he quickly smiled because he enjoyed meeting these charming old ladies with their bubbly personalities and delightful senses of humor.

Born and raised in Tilton, the twin sisters had returned after college to their hometown to assume primary teaching positions in the Wales School—positions they had held for the past forty years. If someone called the sisters "old fashioned, traditional teachers," those who knew them well would classify that as a real understatement. They typified

27

the majority of teachers at Wales, many of whom had already reached retirement age and for years had found a comfortable home at the school. Highly respectful of authority, the sisters were overly courteous in their dealings with Knowles.

As they took their seats, they surprisingly dispensed with their usual small talk. Knowles noticed a nervous, serious look on their usually happy and cherubic faces.

Lucy spoke first in a wavering voice, "Dr. Knowles, thank you so much for meeting with us on such short notice. I don't know where to begin, but we have a situation at the Wales School you need to know about. It concerns our new principal, Ruth Maloney."

Knowles listened intently as Lucy regained her composure and continued.

"In only three months on the job, Ms. Maloney has made us all emotional wrecks."

Knowles interrupted, "When you say all, how many teachers are you talking about?"

"Dr. Knowles, I would say that of the eighteen teachers on our staff, approximately 90% of them are really upset. Morale at Wales is at an all-time low. Ethel and I are not the complaining types. In all our years at Wales, this is the first time we have ever registered a complaint about our principal. Even last spring, when Sally Benton our last principal was forced out, we remained neutral and never spoke out one way or another." Ethel vigorously nodded her head in agreement.

Knowles asked the sisters exactly what Ruth was doing or not doing that was so upsetting to the faculty.

Ethel explained, "In the last few months, she has constantly been in our classrooms, sometimes announced but more often unannounced. She frequently takes over the class, trying to show us some new approaches using curriculum material she has developed for teaching writing and reading comprehension."

"What's wrong with that?" Knowles asked.

"It is the way she does it, Dr. Knowles. She can be very condescending. It is like we are first-year teachers who can't really get it. She will praise you effusively one minute and at another time lash out at you. For example, she saw something she disliked in a classroom the other day and after class she chastised the teacher in the corridor. She has done this several times with different teachers. Other times, she acts sweet and charming. In all my years of teaching, I have never seen a principal act like that. She is like a walking time bomb."

Ethel was really animated at this point. "Dr. Knowles do you remember a character in one of Hemingway's books[9] whom he described as being so unpredictable that you never knew when you were going to be stroked with a velvet glove or hit with a hammer? That is Ruth Maloney." Although surely a rough translation, Knowles got the point.

Knowles informed the two ladies that he would look into the matter without delay. On the way out of his office, Lucy turned and commented, "You have no idea how bad things are at Wales, Dr. Knowles. Ms. Maloney has caused such mass emotional stress, several teachers have taken sick leave for chronic diarrhea."

"I am sorry to hear that Lucy," Knowles sheepishly replied. It was clear he had a serious problem on his hands.

RUTH MALONEY

Ruth Maloney had an interesting background. The oldest of seven children from a devout, financially strapped Irish Catholic family in South Boston, she had attended Catholic schools and learned the family values of hard work and frugality.

Ruth had developed into a tall, rail thin, but attractive woman with penetrating blue eyes. She possessed a keen intelligence and a serious demeanor. She failed, however, to inherit her father's Irish sense of humor and advanced social skills that were frequently on display at the local pub. Instead, she resembled her mother, a gracious and charming lady whose major job was to control her hard working but overly sociable husband. Neighbors described Mrs. Maloney as a serious but lovely lady who was totally devoted to her family and church.

Like many Irish families of that generation, Ruth's parents had high aspirations for their children and encouraged them to seek careers as lawyers, politicians, priests, firemen, policemen, or politicians. In Ruth's case, they encouraged her to become a nun.

Ruth did not resist her parent's urgings. When she began her training as a nun, it was apparent that her academic excellence would allow her to pursue a teaching career and in the process have her undergraduate and graduate degrees paid for by the church. Eventually, she taught in a number of Catholic elementary schools in the Boston area and completed her bachelor's and master's degrees with high honors.

During her doctoral study in reading, Ruth began to take a hard look at her professional future. She yearned for greater independence. What she describes as the "stifling existence" of a nun in a teaching order was getting to her.

There was another motivation as well. Her ambition to become a principal ("only overripe nuns get to be principals in my order") couldn't wait. She noticed that tuition assistance was provided by school districts around Boston and she so badly wanted to finish her doctorate in reading while at the same time making a decent salary.

Ruth left her religious order and made the move to public schools. Driven by her strong work ethic and persistence, she established an enviable record as a reading specialist. She also completed her doctoral program in short order. At her school, she displayed such leadership potential that when a principal vacancy occurred, she was the hands down choice for the job.

Success as a principal, however, is not automatically bestowed on a teacher simply because she was an esteemed faculty colleague before ascending to the principal's throne. Professional staff jealousy, lack of objectivity because of your own personal biases, misuse of your new authority as a result of inexperience, and perceived relationship changes by others all contribute to problems in the transition from being a teacher "in the ranks" to becoming the new boss.

Ruth easily averted these problems. She was very confident and comfortable in her new role. She knew and respected the strengths and abilities of her teachers. She understood their needs and how to motivate those who needed motivating. After all, she had been the reading consultant in their classrooms and had already established effective working relationships with them.

On the flip side, the teachers knew Ruth well and were not bothered by some of her idiosyncrasies. They respected and admired her knowledge and rich background in reading and appreciated her passion for achieving student success. They accepted her leadership style and appreciated her assistance in their classrooms. As a result, Ruth flourished for a decade as principal in this high-achieving school.

TILTON BECKONS

When the Tilton search committee toured Ruth's school, they discovered that teachers were using a reading program that Ruth has recently published. Student test scores in reading and language arts were at all-time highs and teachers praised Ruth as an exceptional instructional leader. Ruth frequently traveled throughout the country promoting her reading program and giving teacher workshops. The demand for her services was high and the consultant money was welcomed.

Now at age forty-eight, Ruth was leaving her secure position and accepting a more lucrative offer from Tilton. In her finalist interview, Ruth was asked why she wanted to leave her current position. She gave the standard pat answer, "It is time for a new challenge. I have taken my school to a new level of excellence. I can now leave with a real sense of fulfillment."

Such words make school board members smile. The hidden reason, however, had more to do with money and less responsibility in a considerably smaller school with more resources.

The increase in salary would help support the forthcoming purchase of her new dream house. Ruth saw the smaller school responsibility as an opportunity to satisfy her publisher and allow her more time to pursue her part-time career as a reading consultant and author.

UNHAPPINESS AT WALES

Knowles' first order of business was to validate the Briggs sisters' story. The problems they described had to be exaggerated. After all, the two sisters had never been professionally challenged in over forty years! They must be overreacting!

Knowles walked into Wales and observed how the building looked like a 19th-century schoolhouse with its old, uneven wooden floors and bolted desks. He saw two teachers on each grade level busy talking at kids or having students quietly doing paper work at their desks. He glanced at the combination cafeteria/gym and wondered if it had been built in the Jim Thorpe era.

He met the long-term custodian and asked him if the old boiler would make it until it is replaced in the spring. He was struck by how everything in the building reeked of old age. He thought of the many things in the school that needed updating if it were to be functional in the 21st century.

Wales Elementary was situated in the far end of town and in recent years new expensive homes had sprung up on pastures where dairy cows used to roam. The school could barely accommodate the growing number of students from the new neighborhood. Space was at a premium and class sizes were getting larger.

School officials wanted to close the school and relocate students in a new wing planned for a newer and larger elementary school in the town center. The affluent Wales parents successfully defeated this action and now were demanding that a new classroom wing be added to Wales. Most parents liked the personalization of Wales and didn't object to the structured, traditional teaching philosophy of its faculty. They got to know the teachers well. The superintendent and the school board, however, questioned continuing the status quo because of a need they saw for curriculum and instructional improvement.

Knowles was surprised and a bit leery when Ruth quickly accepted the principal's position at Wales. School board members, however, were elated. He sensed that Ruth's personality might clash with Wales's teachers. He wondered if she could adjust to their traditional mode of thinking and teaching. He prayed that her experience would allow her to carefully develop an effective plan for change. Ruth confidently assured him that she could do this when he asked her during her final interview.

Knowles kept his doubts to himself. Unfortunately, he actually had little choice but to go along with the appointment because Ruth's qualifications and record of success were far superior to those of other candidates.

When three board members visited Ruth's previous school, they were enthused with the creative and successful teaching and learning they observed. It was almost as if they thought that Ruth could transplant that type of success at Wales overnight. Knowles knew better and wondered if the Wales faculty would embrace change that quickly and easily.

SERIOUS TROUBLE AT WALES

Knowles didn't find Ruth in her office, so he walked around the school until he found her leaving a classroom. She greeted him warmly and asked him to tour other classrooms with her. When he asked how things were going, he noticed tenseness in her voice. "Change is coming slowly but it is coming. I am taking everything one step at a time."

Knowles asked if she could stop by his office and chat more in detail with him later in the week.

Prior to his meeting with Ruth, Knowles managed to gather feedback from several credible Wales teachers (some of whom were recommended by the sisters), the school psychologist, and itinerant teachers who were in and out of the school weekly. Unfortunately, the sisters were right; Wales was in serious trouble.

The next day, Knowles received a call from June Street, the board chair.

"Steve, several of us have received phone calls from concerned Wales teachers and parents. They report that a real feud has developed between Ruth and her faculty. What is going on?"

Knowles swallowed hard and explained the events of recent days. He indicated that he was in the fact-finding stage of his investigation and would communicate with the board after speaking with Ruth in detail.

The meeting with Ruth did not go well. He found her very defensive and soured by a "bunch of crybabies" who, she claimed, were teaching in the dark ages and just "putting in their time." Although she kept her professional bearing, he noticed a controlled anger in her voice. Knowles was worried.

"Ruth, do you think you can turn this situation around? Change with this group of teachers will not come easily. Several teachers are saying that your reading program is being stuffed down their throats."

Exasperated, Ruth rose abruptly and looked sternly at Knowles, "Dr. Knowles, all the Wales teachers know is skill and drill, workbooks, workbooks, and more workbooks. It is very discouraging. Most of them have closed minds and resent everything I say to them. They are a spoiled group of people." Before he could respond, Ruth quickly left his office, leaving a bewildered Knowles wondering if the situation could ever be salvaged.

PLAN OF ACTION

Knowles met with his assistant superintendent, his human resources director, and long-time director of student services. Beginning a brainstorming session, he asks, "What is our next step at Wales, gang? I have a school in crisis, a faculty that is intimidated, and a principal who thinks she is faultless and appears inflexible."

Harriet Peckham, the director of student services, spoke first. "After reviewing all this, I agree that the crisis is real. Yelling, screaming, and crying will be next. Something has to be done to bring peace to the school and it has to be done now."

"What about bringing in a professional consultant to work with both sides," suggested Hal Brooks, the human resources director. "I know of an excellent person named Beth Crothers who has done this type of consulting in the private sector, especially with church congregations. This lady has a fine track record in mediating and helping resolve disputes of this nature."

Knowles thought the idea had merit. At least he had a recommendation to make to the school board.

Beth Crothers checked out as a good choice and Ruth appeared to like her. The school board agreed to pay Beth to spend the next month in Wales helping diffuse and hopefully resolve the volatile situation. She agreed to periodically give progress reports to Knowles who would then privately relay this information to the board.

Over the first two weeks, Beth conducted private sessions with teachers, parents, and Ruth. She sensed that Ruth had given up, feeling she was in an incredible sterile situation and had made a bad choice in accepting the Wales job. She even implied that she wanted out as soon as possible.

Beth questioned Ruth's capacity and willingness to change her attitude and approach with resistant teachers. Ruth had never failed before and was shaken terribly, placing the blame on ignorant teachers. Her position hardened over the course of the discussions with Beth. She strongly resented any implication from Beth that she lacked patience or was emotionally threatening to teachers.

Beth reported another reality. There was a minority of teachers who fiercely fought change at Wales. They were opinion leaders in the school and successfully blocked other teachers who might have been open to the changes in methodology being pushed by Ruth. If only Ruth would stop strong-arming them, slow down, and give them more time.

THE BUY OUT

After Beth completed her month in the Wales Elementary, she presented Knowles and the board with a written report and recommendation. When she discussed it with him, she frankly admitted that irreconcilable differences existed between Ruth and her staff and that divorce was the only option. She urged Knowles to meet with Ruth to discuss a possible contract buy-out. Ruth had hinted that she was willing to resign if a satisfactory financial settlement could be reached.

Knowles followed Beth's advice and immediately set up a meeting with Ruth. In recent days, he had received a number of letters from teachers and parents urging him not to renew Ruth's contract. Some suggested that she be asked to resign immediately. He wondered how she was holding up under this siege.

The meeting with Ruth was short and sweet. She was all business and requested a private session with the school board to discuss a settlement. Knowles noticed how tired and beaten she looked. The energy she usually exuded was missing. She asked Knowles for a letter of recommendation and thanked him for his efforts. In a soft voice she said, "Coming here was a huge mistake. It was like coming out of heaven and stepping into hell. I need to get out."

Ruth chose not to hire a lawyer. Instead, she brought a woman friend to the meeting. The board was gracious and gentle with Ruth and reached a fair settlement quickly. Ruth apologized for the problems at Wales; however, the board admitted that they and the Wales staff had to share the blame. As Ruth and her friend left the meeting, Knowles wondered what he was going to do with the Wales situation now.

CASE ANALYSIS

Forget for a moment that the search committee, the school board, and Ruth had blinders on and didn't foresee potential problems at Wales. Their miscalculations are indeed shocking. The appointment by the superintendent and school board of a school leader like Ruth at Wales was a mismatch of the highest order. Only in hindsight can we appreciate the serious blunder that was made, although we can understand the reasons why it happened.

Given the information received, the ranking of applicants by the search committee, school visits to Ruth's previous school that impressed Tilton people, and her interviews where Ruth's charm and intelligence hid some of her interpersonal limitations, most school committees would have made the same decision. Hindsight is wonderful. Unfortunately, we learn from it while our wounds heal slowly from our momentous mistakes.

Two essential questions emerge from this case: Why was Ruth incapable of coping with the unique challenge presented by Wales? And what type of principal could possibly succeed in a school like Wales?

WHY DID RUTH FAIL?

It is easy to blame Ruth's failure solely on her past religious training. People use stereotypical language to describe ex-priests and nuns who have difficulty with the transition from religious careers to public school teaching and school administration.

Adjectives like *inflexible, controlling, tyrannical, punitive,* and *dogmatic* are used frequently. It is a bias that is shared by many administrators involved in the hiring of school personnel. However, this is too simplistic a bias and it also is not true.

Most religious people become fine public school teachers and administrators. Ruth, in fact, had been an excellent, achieving principal in her previous school.

What then led to her demise?

It was a combination of factors, which, when added to Ruth's training and experience as a nun, helped form her unique personality and leadership style. Her family's values and influence as a child; her sense of self-importance gained from being a bright woman who achieved a high level of academic and professional success; and her personality that shaped a leadership style that worked well for her in her previous school but was a bust at Wales.

Ruth was totally unprepared for the Wales experience. In the past, she had never had to build positive group relationships in a strange school setting. In her first principalship, she had already earned status and respect as a teacher in her school. Her teaching colleagues knew her well and accepted her for who she was—a talented professional colleague they had worked well with for years. At Wales, she knew no one and didn't take the time to develop essential interpersonal relationships that are so crucial to a new principal's acceptance and ability to build trust over time.

Ruth also did not have the capacity and skill to build healthy relationships with the type of teacher she found at Wales. Her petulance contributed to the intensity of her conflict with Wales's teachers. She had never met teachers who were so out of touch with contemporary educational practice. The intellectual gap between her and the faculty was considerable. By being critical and expressing disappointment with teacher performance early in her tenure, it was just a matter of time before teachers turned against her. All it took was one outburst or harsh word to a respected fellow teacher to alienate the majority of the faculty.

Unfortunately, Ruth was extremely impatient and had difficulty keeping her emotions under control. Her initial displays of dissatisfaction and upset intimidated teachers.

Many teachers were overwhelmed with her change initiatives and felt threatened. Her zeal in having the staff use her reading program was also problematic. Pushing her program on teachers so soon was a mistake. Many resent outsiders, especially a new principal who has all the answers and does not value their opinions. Ruth reacted badly to this resistance by taking it personally.

Ruth also had no real constituency with parents because she was new to the school. Parents didn't really know her yet and were being fed by the rumor mill generated by teachers—and obviously parents did know the Wales teachers well.

When teachers are unhappy, parents know it. Understandably, they don't want unhappy teachers teaching their children. Surprisingly, Wales's parents were not calling for change and were generally satisfied with the school. The superintendent and school board who clearly saw the need for instructional improvement do not share their feelings. Why this gap in understanding?

With direct assistance from the superintendent and other professionals, Ruth needed to adopt a long-range strategy to educate and convince teachers that the proposed changes would be beneficial to their students. Ruth also needed to educate parents on the changes at Wales and ask for their support. Because of Ruth's intimidating style, this type of process never occurred. Unfortunately, all parents heard were rumblings from teachers about the tyrant of a principal that Knowles and the school board had hired.

Superintendent Knowles didn't help Ruth's situation either. Why didn't he know about the crisis at Wales earlier?

He knew that Wales would present a major challenge to any new principal. It is one thing to lack the courage to communicate your concerns with Ruth's appointment and another thing to not take measures to have open and active lines of communication with her in her first few months on the job. His lack of presence directly contributed to Ruth's troubles.

Knowles' crisis intervention plan was also too little, too late. Critical damage in relationships was beyond repair by the time he followed up on the Briggs sisters' complaint.

Knowles' failure was in not having a well-thought-out induction plan in place before Ruth began her responsibilities. He also needed to be personally invested in the plan. A major error on his part was assuming that an experienced principal, or any principal for that matter, would not need immediate and continuing support at Wales.

CAN ANY PRINCIPAL SUCCEED AT WALES?

Finally, can a principal with the right personality and style succeed at Wales?

A crisis could have been averted if the school board had hired a good old boy from the faculty to manage the school. This sounds ridiculous, but in actuality, that is what happened when the board made an interim appointment providing Wales with a cooling-off period before starting another search later in the year.

Hiring a manager type and continuing the status quo at Wales is not the long-range answer. Because it would take a good period of time to realize school improvement, Wales needed a principal who knew how to bond with teachers. This had to be the first priority. This principal would have to be a visionary leader who could genuinely involve teachers and parents in developing a strategic plan of improvement.

A new principal will definitely need consensus building skills. He will also need to convince everyone that the details of the improvement plan are not the priority, but the contributions of teachers and parents in the plan's development are.

Creating joint ownership of the plan will be crucial. In short, it should be about the principal building positive and trusting relationships with Wales's teachers and parents and working together with a common agenda.

The Wales's principal will also need humility. A principal who can sincerely say, "I want to listen to your ideas about some things we can improve on at Wales. Many of you have been here a long time and have good insights about the students and their needs. I need your help." A principal who will be a credible, supportive leader and will listen well before speaking will gain respect and will significantly increase his chances for success at Wales.

You would have expected Ruth to have a high level of humility. However, even as a nun, she had never been in a position requiring humility. She had conquered every situation and challenge in her life. Her vision of leadership was extremely narrow and her leadership style limited. Her emotional makeup left her little room to adapt to the Wales challenge. Her answer was to escape as soon as she could. She realized that she was in the wrong place. Leaving was a good idea.

Today, Ruth is a highly successful author of reading books and serves as a consultant to numerous school districts throughout the country.

7

Behind Closed Doors: The Case of Judd Silva, Respected Superintendent of Schools

MAN IN THE SPOTLIGHT

When she called for a vote to go into executive session, Sheila Wroneski, newly elected chairlady of the Tremble School Committee, let out a sigh of relief. The local reporters covering the school board meeting were itching to leave the boardroom to find a quiet place to fine-tune the emerging articles on their laptops.

It was a newsworthy meeting. The school board had issued the results of their annual performance evaluation of superintendent of schools, Judd Silva. Silva was completing his first year on the job and the board had rated him "excellent" in every evaluative category. Sheila then had the other four board members make comments about Judd's first year accomplishments.

Dennis Fitzgerald set the tone, "Judd Silva has done a tremendous job in a very difficult year. His positive relationship with the board, teachers, parents, and members of the community is remarkable considering the short time he has been with us." A reporter whispered to one of his colleagues, "This sounds like a real love-in to me."

Sitting on a side table with his assistant superintendent, Ellen Grass, Judd squirmed in his seat. He didn't like public praise and knew that the board's evaluation was shoddily done. It was a paper-and-pencil exercise with the data summarized by Sheila. There was no formal evaluative conference with Judd prior to the public release of the board's report, other than a side comment one day by Sheila, who hinted that he would be pleased with the evaluation.

Judd agreed with Dennis's reference to a difficult year. It was an incredibly difficult year, probably one of his most challenging ever. The suicide of a high school junior, a contentious termination of an elementary principal, and a highly publicized sexual assault charge against a male elementary teacher who had allegedly molested a third grade female student were but a few of the notable incidents that marked Judd's first year in Tremble.

Judd listened to the remaining board members sing his praises, wondering what they would say if they knew his feelings about their performance. He thought about how crazy life was. The board felt he did an excellent job while his opinion of the board's performance was that it was dirt poor. They apparently had no idea about the frustration that he had with their collective performance.

After the regular portion of their meeting ended, the board reconvened in a closed, private session "to discuss issues with respect to the character and reputation of personnel." After discussing pending litigation involving the recently dismissed elementary principal, Sheila said, "Judd, all of us are pleased to have you as our superintendent. The Tremble students and teachers are fortunate to have such a highly qualified and competent leader. However, there is a small concern we would like to bring to your attention. I'll let Dennis explain." "Judd, we notice that you tend to bristle every time we offer you advice or disagree with your position on things. Why do you do that?"

After giving a feeble response about his ingrained habits, Judd swallowed hard and thought, "Maybe they do know what I think about them after all."

JUDD'S DISCONTENT

Prior to accepting the Tremble job, Judd Silva had had an enviable twenty-four-year record of achievement as an educator. Appointed to his first superintendent's position at age thirty-one, he was so respected that he twice had been a finalist for state education commissioner positions in two different states. He was well known in his state and region having served as chair of numerous prestigious professional organizations.

Judd's leadership as superintendent was exemplary in his three previous school districts. One past school board member paid him the ultimate compliment; "Judd Silva is a unique and gifted leader. He is extremely competent and ably led our district to new heights of success and achievement."

Because Judd continually sought new challenges, his service in three different states created future retirement problems due to lack of retirement portability. At age forty-eight, he realized that it was time to think about life after the superintendency. He was completing nearly ten years in his current position in New Hampshire and this was the maximum time that he could transfer to Massachusetts, the state where he was vested.

When the Tremble vacancy occurred, it made perfect sense to apply for the position. A medium-size district in Central Massachusetts, Tremble schools had an excellent reputation. Lately, enrollment decline was becoming a problem creating a need to deal with the tricky business of shifting enrollment and reorganizing grades throughout the district.

Tremble parents were proud of their schools. School budget support was consistently strong as evidenced by impressive per pupil cost figures. The town was one of the more attractive suburbs in Worcester County drawing middle- and upper middle-class families. Tremble also paid its superintendent well.

However, Judd had mixed feelings about accepting the Tremble job. He was getting tired of the superintendent's job, especially the increasing pressure and accountability. It was a job with no real constituency and you were always in the public limelight dodging one crisis after another. It was a job that slowly wore you down. Many times, your tenure was only as long as the next board election.

Although he was relatively happy in his present position, he had no choice but to leave. He would have to work as a superintendent for another seventeen years to receive full retirement benefits in New Hampshire. That meant thirty-three years as a school superintendent! Of course, he had to live that long, too.

There was another reason he was reluctant to leave New Hampshire.

Judd's youngest son was in his junior year in high school. An all-state quarterback, he was already being recruited by major college football programs. Consequently, he wanted his family to remain in New Hampshire until his son graduated. He must find a school board that will be understanding and not insist that he relocate in their community for at least two years. He found that school board in Tremble.

THE FIRST YEAR

As a seasoned superintendent, Judd knew that, in his first year, gaining board acceptance and confidence in his leadership were priorities. He limited proposing any major change initiatives and concentrated on doing some solid strategic planning. As he worked for board acceptance, he reached out to teachers, parents, and community leaders. He asked many questions, listened intently, and sought advice. He created a district newsletter solely to feature the good things happening in Tremble schools. He praised teachers and the creative activities he observed as he visited classrooms. Although dangerous with a hammer, he joined a group of parents that built an impressive playground at one of the elementary schools. And finally, he worked to bond with his principals and central office administrators and gain their respect and support.

Judd also tried to get the school board to make some procedural changes. He sensitively approached the board and suggested they eliminate some minor areas of responsibility and delegate some of those decisions to him. The traditionally voluminous agenda that guaranteed a minimum of four-hour board meetings was shortened somewhat as the board reluctantly agreed to a consent agenda for some business previously requiring their separate vote and discussion.

Judd was surprised that the board was not more receptive to delegating some of their mundane responsibilities to him but when they balked at some of his suggestions, he backed off. Then again, it was not surprising that they accused him of bristling on occasion. After all, he could only keep so much of his frustration with their stubbornness and need for control under cover.

There was another board practice and tradition that irked Judd. After lengthy meetings, the board adjourned to the local pub for a drink or two. Most members usually attended the sessions, but Sheila and Karen, the vice-chairlady, never missed the opportunity for this informal bull session.

At first, Judd felt socially compelled to join the group for a drink. Over time, he found it made him uncomfortable when Sheila and Karen continued the habit of grilling him about school matters—especially with other board members within listening range. The two women were particularly interested in the schools their children attended. They delved into private matters relating to teachers and administrators that Judd felt were inappropriate. After several of these pub sessions, Judd realized he had an ethical problem on his hands.

Eventually, Judd refused the board's invitations for "pub talk. " He offered excuses like having a need to stay behind to finish important paperwork that couldn't wait or being too exhausted and in need of a good night's rest. He realized that his absence gave the board an opportunity to talk about him but really didn't care as long as he could avoid further cornering by Sheila and her cohort, Karen. As his first year in Tremble came to an end, Judd realized that he would have continuing difficulty working for this board unless some major changes were made.

YEAR TWO

As his second year began, Judd became more aggressive in his attempt to increase his decision-making authority. He wouldn't continue to be just an expensive administrative clerk to the board. He had reached a point when just being the "good soldier" must end.

He didn't care if the board got upset with his trying to wrestle some authority away from them. More subtle approaches hadn't worked. He had always been an influential chief executive officer with sufficient authority to make significant decisions, and failure to have this authority would weaken his ability to make changes and seek improvement.

His strong leadership style had always worked in his previous positions. Without more executive authority, he knew his effectiveness would be limited and he couldn't live with that situation. The Tremble School Board was definitely a different breed of cat and, based upon his first-year experience, he feared that they might be incapable of making fundamental changes in the way they operated.

Down deep, Judd was bothered by something else, something that had been burning inside his head and his heart during the past few years. He was starting to sicken with the thought of spending the rest of his professional life as a school superintendent. The Tremble experience was materially contributing to this disenchantment. At times, his feelings were so intense that he started contemplating career changes, especially job opportunities in New Hampshire.

In addition, Judd wouldn't miss the boring 84-mile commute back and forth to his New Hampshire home on weekends or those lonely nights spent in the dreary room he rented in Tremble during the work week. On the other hand, he was willing to live in Tremble if things worked out. He liked the people, especially the teachers and administrators. He also liked the town's attractive residential sub-divisions, its proximity to Boston and Worcester, and its New England charm. Unfortunately, relocation was out of the question unless the growing schism between him and the board reversed itself soon.

THE BOARD'S DISCONTENT

As a matter of routine, Sheila and Karen scheduled a meeting every Monday morning with Judd. The nearly two-hour sessions had been initiated during the previous superintendent's tenure. This time provided an opportunity to develop the monthly board agenda and to exchange information, making both women better informed about what was happening in the schools. Judd always wondered why the ladies also needed to have their pub discussions in addition to the Monday morning sessions.

It was obvious that both ladies enjoyed their new authority as school board leaders. Both were young at-home mothers living in the same neighborhood where their children attended the same elementary school.

Sheila and Karen had time on their hands and took their new responsibilities very seriously—too seriously if you asked Judd. Their new roles provided them with status and recognition in the community. They also got most of their information through tales provided by their children or the town rumor mill. Both ladies were known to set time records on the telephone chatting with acquaintances about school-related matters. Most of this information was passed on to Judd every Monday morning before he pointedly asked the ladies to discuss the professional items that were listed on their agenda.

Both women were also quite friendly with Judd's assistant superintendent, Ellen Grass. Ellen was a bright, ambitious woman who would soon be looking for her own superintendent's position. She had been in Tremble for four years with responsibility for curriculum and instruction. She was very knowledgeable and capable. Sheila and Karen had plugged Ellen into their pipeline long before Judd Silva arrived on the scene.

In a Monday morning session in late fall, Sheila and Karen indicated they needed to share some concerns with Judd. Sheila began, "Judd, Karen and I and other board members wonder how happy you are in Tremble. We have noticed an increasing feistiness and impatience in your manner and we are concerned."

Judd candidly explained his frustration with the board's reluctance to give him greater independence and authority, "I feel a bit suffocated here, Sheila. We have some major differences in operational philosophy and the respective lines of authority between the board and the superintendent. I have stated this to board members on several occasions and have made suggestions on how we can better define our roles. To date, I haven't seen any reception to my recommendations."

"You need to give us time," Sheila countered. "Remember, we have been conditioned by Ed (the former superintendent). We agreed to a consent agenda, didn't we? We are trying hard, Judd, give us a chance."

Karen picked up the conversation, "Sheila and I are also concerned with your personal life. Traveling back and forth to New Hampshire has to take its toll on you, Judd. When are you going to buy a house in Tremble?"

Karen's question really irritated Judd. "I told the board that I would relocate in Tremble in two years and you hired me with that understanding. I am waiting for my son to graduate this coming June. As far as my personal life is concerned, it is fine, thank you. "

As Sheila and Karen abruptly left the meeting, Judd wondered if this was the beginning of the end.

PAINFUL CAPE COD

The opportunity for Judd and the board's continuing discussion about its growing disagreements occurred unexpectedly a few weeks later at a joint conference of superintendents and school boards on Cape Cod.

Judd was in his motel after the day's activities. It was 10:15 p.m. and he was taking a steamy, hot tub bath to ease a painful cyst in his groin when the phone rang. Dripping wet, he grabbed the phone. It was Sheila. "Judd, could you come to room 318? All of us are here and would like to talk to you." Judd was so shocked by the late-night call that he forgot to ask Sheila what the board wanted to talk about.

Ten minutes later, Judd entered room 318 and immediately noticed the serious looks on the faces of board members. They were sitting in a semi circle and asked Judd to take a seat in front of them. Judd felt as if he were either in front of a grand jury or being readied for a firing squad. It was surreal.

Led by Sheila, Karen, and Dennis (he lamely tried to provide some comic relief), the board literally interrogated Judd for the next two hours. Judd felt a great need for a defense attorney. The three board members were quite animated while the other two board members sat passively, appearing very uncomfortable with the dialogue.

Sheila and Karen acted like scorned women explaining how depressed they were with the deteriorating relations between Judd and themselves. "How can you act with such disdain toward us?" Sheila asked.

Judd responded that it wasn't disdain but more frustration with the board's misunderstanding of its policy role. He then mounted a counter-attack.

Judd offered his explanation of what he meant by policy-making as distinguished from administration, an area he contended should rightfully be left to the superintendent. "In my years as superintendent I have never had board members so closely looking over my shoulder, questioning everything I do and say. I realize last year was pressure packed with much controversy, however, I ask you to evaluate how well I handled those problems. Did I not consult with you and ask for your input when it was needed? In spite of this, you were still not satisfied and felt left out. Do you need to make every decision? Wasn't my performance evaluation last year truthful and valid? I honestly wonder at times if you even need a superintendent in Tremble."

Judd's last comment upset Sheila and she retaliated quickly, "Judd, you are having difficulty understanding that you work for us. We do not work for you. We have a legal and fiduciary responsibility as an elected body and will not give that authority away."

Judd responded, "God, you just don't get it."

Sheila continued, "We have recently heard some things that are upsetting to us. We were told that you had Jim Owens, our high school technology teacher, make a highlight football video of your son's football games. How can you justify using school personnel for something like that?"

Karen jumped in as well. "We have also noticed that your car is not in the office parking lot after 2:30 p.m. on Friday afternoons. Are you leaving early to go home to New Hampshire for the weekend?" With a menacing look on his face, Judd strongly responded, "I don't need to listen to this petty stuff. Good night."

At this point, he realized that the situation was hopeless. The throbbing cyst in his groin was not nearly as painful as the sharp, piercing words of the two ladies. He looked at his watch after he returned to his room. It was 12:25 a.m.

DECISION TO RESIGN

A week passed and Judd thought constantly about his future. What should he do?

He was midway through the second year of his three-year contract and realized if he resigned now he would have to explain to perspective future employers why he worked in Tremble such a short time. He also needed to complete two years of service in Tremble in order to gain eligibility for Massachusetts's retirement.

He struggled with his dilemma. Deep in his soul, he knew he couldn't complete his full contract obligation and seriously questioned if he could even complete the four remaining months in this, his second year.

Judd didn't fear adverse action by the board to terminate him, but he was convinced that it was unlikely at this point they would renew his contract when it expired in sixteen months unless some miracle occurred. He reasoned that it might be prudent to delay any precipitous action to resign immediately and back-step to avoid any future confrontations with the board. This would leave him time to check out professor vacancies and other job options for next fall in the New Hampshire area.

The residue left by the Cape Cod fiasco still resonated inside his gut, but Judd contained himself and worked to heal the strained relationship with the board. His changed attitude and cooperation encouraged board members. In their minds, the crisis with their superintendent had passed. Judd, however, was still miserable but kept his unhappiness hidden. He knew the time was approaching when he had to make a decision regarding his future in Tremble.

One early March morning, Judd woke up at 4:30 a.m. and looked out his dirty apartment window at the falling snow. The landscape was a glossy white so typical of a New England snowfall. The beauty of the snow escaped Judd because it represented a part of his job he hated. Canceling school was always risky business and affected hundreds of families. For eighteen years he had detested this responsibility— especially when it was a close call like this morning. It was a part of the job that really couldn't be delegated. Business managers and police and fire chiefs only advised, but it was the superintendent who was responsible for the ultimate decision.

As he glanced out the window, Judd suddenly realized what he had to do about Tremble. He would resign effective at the end of the school year in June and seek a buy-out of the third year of his contract. He now knew that his need to escape from Tremble was as much caused by his growing dislike of the job of school superintendent as it was the oppressive and dominating Tremble School Board.

A SURPRISE ENDING

Tremble teachers, parents, and the general public had no idea that their superintendent was about to resign. After all, the conflict between Judd and the board had been hidden behind closed doors because it was the sort of "dirty linen" that Sheila and Karen kept to themselves.

The buy-out of Judd's contract was handled in private session as well. The lawyer from the state superintendents' association represented Judd and met with the Tremble board and their attorney as Judd sat in his outer office. His lawyer went back and forth between the boardroom and Judd attempting to negotiate a joint settlement. Avoiding the sensitive details, Judd's lawyer simply told the board that Judd was unhappy in Tremble and wished to leave in June. The board asked him to reconsider but he refused and eventually a settlement was reached, where he received about half of this third-year salary.

POST SCRIPT

When the news of Judd's resignation became public, the newspapers quoted Judd's politically correct comments about his philosophical differences with the board relating to roles and responsibilities. Sheila commented about Judd not being happy in Tremble.

The public reaction was one of surprise and confusion. "What are the real reasons?" "I thought Silva was very highly valued by everyone?"

Unfortunately, the detailed story of the bitterness, mutual disenchantment, and breakdown of the relationship between Judd and the board could never be told because it involved personality conflicts, questions of professional ethics, and ugly power scenes better left unreported.

Two noteworthy incidents occurred after Judd's resignation. The first concerned a scene at the annual town meeting in April when a citizen asked the board, "Madame chair, why is it that you are losing an obviously competent superintendent after only two years? I have heard nothing but compliments about his work here." Sheila's pathetically vacuous response was recognized as such by the audience of 500 people as Judd sat quietly enjoying the egg form on Sheila's face.

The second incident was more disturbing and suspicious. Ellen Grass was appointed as Judd's successor a few weeks after his resignation without a board search. Ellen had already signed a contract as a new superintendent in a Connecticut community a week prior to Judd's surprising resignation. Although Ellen had known of Judd's dissatisfaction with the board, he never shared his intent to resign with her. He had been careful in what he said to Ellen. Ellen's close relationship with Sheila and Karen bothered him because he wondered what information she might have shared with the two women.

Although Judd lacked any concrete proof of disloyalty, he left Tremble wondering what role, if any, Ellen had played in his difficulties with the board. The fact that Ellen reneged on a signed contract in Connecticut and accepted the Tremble offer was a sign to Judd that she must have wanted his job badly. Interestingly, Ellen only lasted a short time in the Tremble job before permanently relocating in Connecticut.

As for Judd, he rebounded well, moving into higher education for the remainder of his career, where he enjoyed considerable success.

CASE ANALYSIS

There are several key factors that contributed to the conflict between Judd and the board.

The Tremble board did not hire the type of superintendent it really wanted. They were smitten by Judd's record of achievement, his articulateness, and his apparent political savvy. They knew Judd's professional credentials would impress their constituents, and this was important to their public image. However, they overestimated their ability to direct someone with the strong and confident style of Judd Silva. It was a major misread on their part.

They should have hired a novice superintendent who would be more open to their direction and would do what they wanted him to do. There was little room in Tremble for the independent-thinking type. The board needed a school leader who was way beyond collaboration, someone who would constantly seek them out for advice before making decisions. They needed a person who would follow the practice of the past superintendent and flood them with memos that report every little detail of school developments. Instead, it hired a Judd Silva.

Judd's initial success and popularity contributed to his conflict with the board. First, it provided Judd with the self-confidence and momentum to aggressively push the board for changes in their modus operandi. Secondly, Judd's quick popularity threatened the board. They feared a loss in power and influence. This was definitely bothersome to a group with their particular collective personality. These factors provided toxic fuel to the developing breach between Judd and board members.

The board also had unusual difficulty changing the habits and practices it had enjoyed during the tenure of the previous superintendent. It relished its pub gossip sessions, its artful micromanaging, and its excessive preoccupation with seeing school problems and issues mainly through the eyes of their children.

Sheila and Karen were very naïve because of their inexperience. Although they passionately controlled the board, they misunderstood their role and responsibilities as chairlady and vice-chairlady. They behaved more like watchdogs and in-house critics, rather than as Judd's supporters and colleagues sharing mutually held goals.

The school board needed to assert their authority at every turn and couldn't see the necessity of giving Judd the professional distance and independence he needed and wanted. They were incapable of subjugating their own strong need to control and direct their "subordinate." They resisted any attempt to relinquish the authority that they enjoyed under the previous superintendent. As Sheila repeated on a number of occasions, they wanted to make it clear that the superintendent worked for them and not the other way around.

Judd resisted the board's attempt to "own him" (his words). Prior to Tremble, Judd had worked for nineteen years with more than thirty different board members in three communities. He told many of his friends that he had never seen a more condescending group of people than the Tremble board.

Judd admitted that he harbored a growing personal dislike for Sheila and Karen. He knew they probably sensed his negative feelings toward them. This clearly didn't help their relationship. He saw the women as incorrigible, devious, and manipulative. They probably thought he was power hungry, overly sensitive, and impatient.

There was no question that Judd did not have the patience with the Tremble board that he did with his previous boards. Those boards were less threatened with his style. They trusted him and realized his need for administrative authority.

With Tremble, his tolerance level was definitely low. Although experienced with considerable political savvy, he had never faced the type of unique challenge presented by Sheila, Karen, and Dennis. When he looked around the table at past boards, he saw the chair as a friend and a majority of board members as active supporters of his leadership. In Tremble, he saw mainly antagonists at the table.

The board obviously thought he had a superior attitude and had all the answers. His inability to successfully educate the board in his first year created a degree of frustration he could not tolerate.

But he would not be a lackey to the board. He would not sacrifice any of his long-held principles. If the board would not change, then he was out the door. Call it impatience and egocentricity if you will, but he believed, "They need me, more than I need them." This type of attitude didn't help the situation.

Judd blamed himself for not doing more detailed research on board members before accepting the Tremble job. He was totally fooled by their initial charm and graciousness and became overly influenced by the huge salary jump and the solving of his retirement dilemma. What a mistake he had made! Now he found himself trying to end the misery in the most graceful and intelligent way possible.

Judd also overestimated his ability to be content with being separated from his family and friends. It was the first time in his career that he was away from his wife and children for such long stretches. He missed the daily interactions with his sons and daughters and that contributed to his unhappiness in Tremble.

Judd also felt guilty for not being honest about his own feelings. His disenchantment with the superintendent's job was a major contributor to his difficulties in Tremble. In the past, he had cringed when friends suggested he might be experiencing burnout and quickly went into denial.

If he had not been harboring this growing dislike for the superintendent's job, he might have been more patient with the Tremble board, giving it more time to come around. Might his strong desire to retire and head into another career direction have created these same problems with his old board or another board in another town other than Tremble?

Judd still searches for answers to that question. But he is sure about one thing. His decision to become Tremble superintendent was such an incredibly poor choice that it definitely hastened his decision to make a career change.

8

Conclusions

THE FAILURE OF SEARCH COMMITTEES
AND SCHOOL BOARDS

In the three cases in this book, it is obvious that local search committees and school boards materially contributed to the failures of Becky Hazard, Ruth Maloney, and Judd Silva.

Although an impressive candidate, Becky's leadership style was the exact opposite of what was needed at the Pleasantville Elementary School. Becky's lack of administrative experience made it more difficult for the search committee to gather crucial data; however, enough evidence was available to make some members of the committee skeptical about appointing her.

The long delay in making an appointment was a sign that several committee members were concerned that she might be the wrong fit for the school. Because the vacancy occurred at mid-year, the committee felt compelled to make a recommendation rather than follow the disturbing trend of hiring another interim principal. Appointing her was a risk—a risk that backfired.

In Ruth's case, the school board was more concerned with professional credentials than the specific leadership needs at the Wales Elementary School. The board failed to focus on the unique culture of Wales and anticipate problems a new school leader might have in that culture. Ruth's previous professional experience and accomplishments were very impressive and her ability to present herself as a charming and gracious lady disguised some of her emotional issues. Judd's impressive credentials also swayed the Tremble board. His hiring enhanced the prestige of the board and that was important, especially to the new board chairlady, Sheila Wronoski.

Unfortunately, the Tremble board failed to conduct an honest needs assessment and determine the type of leader they actually wanted and needed. The board, however, might have had difficulty in doing an accurate assessment. A qualified outside consultant could have helped. Such a process, however, could have resulted in the realization that they wanted a new superintendent who was exactly like their old one.

Finally, the board failed to delve more deeply into the reasons for Judd's interest in Tremble and the degree of his desire for the job. The same can be said about Ruth because she, too, disguised her primary reasons for wanting the Wales job.

WOULD A COMPREHENSIVE ASSESSMENT PROCESS MADE ANY DIFFERENCE?

Data from a candidate's psychological and cognitive assessment tests, aligned with a cultural assessment of the schools, and a well-done assessment about the type of leader needed, might have prevented the hiring of the three professionals from occurring, but there is no guarantee of that. Even after careful determination of the type of leader that best matched the organizational culture and needs of a school, school district, or school board, it is conceivable that Becky, Ruth, and Judd might still have been hired.

Why? It is easy to understand. Each had impressive credentials and glowing references. There was no indication that all three were not highly qualified candidates. The school visitations by search committee members produced only positive comments about candidate performance. All three clearly stood out in their applicant pools as the most qualified candidates (This raises questions about the declining quality and quantity of applicants for school leadership positions but that is another story).

None had ever experienced professional failure and had long records of success. All three outdistanced other competitors during the searches. All had the knowledge and technical expertise to be successful in their new jobs. Unfortunately, by themselves, knowledge, technical expertise, and successful past experience were not enough to avoid failure in their new positions.

COMMON ELEMENTS

The case analyses provide details on why all three administrators failed in their new positions and how the schools and school districts failed them. Interestingly, in addition to the misjudgments made by search committees and boards, other common elements in all three cases shed further light on why these apparently qualified leaders experienced crash landings.

Here are some noteworthy commonalties:

1. **All three administrators received minimal support from their superiors.**

Lowe decided to mentor Becky but rejected the idea of hiring an outside mentor. He and the school board knew of the difficulties at Southside Elementary, but overestimated the ability of a promising but novice principal to cope with the unusual challenge the school presented. Lowe's initial advice "to immediately give the school back to the students" placed immediate unrealistic expectations on Becky. His establishment of performance objectives for Becky was not done until she ran into trouble and then the objectives, composed jointly with a disgruntled union, were designed as corrective in nature with her job at stake.

Superintendent Knowles did not share his doubts and concerns about Ruth with the school board before she was hired. He did not provide the board with the type of professional insight that might have delayed her hiring or at least convinced him to establish an induction process where Ruth could receive the initial assistance she desperately needed. Further, he failed to closely observe and communicate with Ruth during her first few weeks on the job and by the time the Briggs sisters alerted him to impending disaster, it was too late. Consequently, hiring a human resource consultant was a waste of money.

Shelia Wronoski misunderstood her role as school board chairlady. She became Judd Silva's resident critic rather than a supporter of his leadership. Based upon their previous experience with Judd's predecessor, Sheila and the vice-chairlady, Karen, enjoyed their perceived positions of control and authority and weren't about to let the school board give any of it away. This attitude created predictable conflict with someone with Judd's leadership style and need for decision-making power.

2. **All three administrators refused to adapt their leadership styles to the unique challenges they faced.**
Each individual lacked patience, stood on principle, and refused to approach change gradually. This stance places all three in uncompromising positions. Rather than showing incredible patience and working with people to establish the conditions for change, they wanted instant change. They wanted to leap and not crawl first. In the final analysis, all three administrators failed to adopt incremental change strategies. They wanted instant success. The negative result was the creation of situations they eventually deemed impossible. Judd and Ruth decided the best way to end their dilemmas was to leave before they were further discredited or terminated. Unfortunately, Becky followed a very public and painful legal route before she left with her settlement.

3. **There was a real mismatch of leader personality of the three administrators with the organizational culture of both elementary schools and the Tremble School Board.**
Becky's authoritative demeanor, Ruth's lack of emotional control and intellectual arrogance, and Judd's need for power and authority immediately clashed with the cultures they confronted.
All three fought the good fight but eventually realized their approaches were not working. Rather than acquiescing, they decided to continue to force their will on others, intensifying their conflicts and reducing their chances for survival.
Judd did suppress his angst and did adopt a more meditative style during his first year and again after his confrontational meeting with the board at Cape Cod. His political savvy was at play on those occasions with his main intent being to make himself look like a victim of an ignorant board.

4. Each school leader accepted their new positions for the wrong reasons.

Although disguised from the search committees, the real reasons for each school leader's decision to seek their new position are material gain, status, and prestige.

These are, of course, somewhat legitimate reasons; however, when used as priorities, these reasons can cause a person to overlook several crucial elements. For example, how carefully did they study and/or understand the organizational cultures they would face? How thoroughly did they reseach the past history of key people they would supervise or work under? Given the leadership styles and personal needs, how well did they evaluate their chances for success? The lack of due diligence was obvious.

It can be argued that Judd didn't want the Tremble position in the first place, but was driven by a desire to solve his retirement dilemma and gain an increase in salary.

Ruth saw the Wales opportunity as a chance for a major salary boost and more time to devote to her budding career as a reading consultant and author.

Becky viewed the Southside opportunity as an opportunity to skip over the job of assistant principal and accept a more prestigious and lucrative position as a principal in her hometown.

5. The quality and type of previous experience the three leaders brought to their new jobs should have been more carefully evaluated by the screening committees and the school boards.

Although Ruth had completed ten successful years as principal in her previous school, the culture of that school was vastly different from that at Wales.

Her staff relationships had already formed before she was appointed at her last school and teachers looked beyond some of her interpersonal limitations because they knew her well and weren't intimidated by her leadership style; whereas, the Wales faculty saw her as a tyrant. The sophistication and background of her previous faculty far surpassed that of the Wales faculty. This situation created an intellectual gap between herself and Wales teachers and became very problematic for Ruth, causing her unusual stress and frustration.

With Becky, it was a case of a lack of supervisory experience and the insecurity that went with that. Although a successful teacher with strong convictions, she lacked the political astuteness and judgment that only comes with leadership experience.

As for Judd, one would think that his long record of success in different communities would have taught him to cope with a controlling board and an inexperienced chair. However, there was another factor at play here, one that caused Judd to complain that he had never experienced a power-hungry board like the type he found in Tremble. A careful look and evaluation of Judd's past experiences would have revealed a telling fact.

Judd's past experience resembled that of a character in Tevanian's novel, *Shibumi*, when one character says to another, "You are like the artisan who boasts about twenty years in his craft while in fact he has only one year of experience, twenty times over."[11]

In other words, Judd had a record of success with past boards that gave him wide latitude in decision making. Tremble was the first board in his experience that refused to relinquish the degree of power and control it had enjoyed in the past. Combined with his growing discontent with the changing role of a superintendent, he chose to resign rather than stay and continue to challenge the mindset of the board and risk possible non-renewal of his contract.

WHAT WOULD THE THEORISTS SAY?

Although a bit presumptuous, it is interesting to speculate what Goleman, Fullan, and Greenleaf might say if they had an opportunity to read the case histories of Becky Hazard, Ruth Maloney, and Judd Silva.

Goleman

Daniel Goleman sees effective leaders as having a high degree of emotional intelligence[12] He uses his theory to explain why highly intelligent and highly skilled leaders when promoted to new positions fail on the job.

Goleman would most likely identify a low level of self-awareness, self-regulation, empathy, and social skill as major contributors to the failure of Becky, Ruth, and Judd.

For example, Goleman describes a leader that is highly aware as someone who understands his or her values and goals. Someone who knows where he is headed and why and is capable of turning down a job offer that is tempting financially but does not fit with his principles or long term goals.[13] Interestingly, the leaders in the three cases all accepted jobs for the wrong reasons with financial gain being the prime motivation.

When discussing empathy, Goleman admits that some people are born with certain levels of empathy and others are not.[14] He is uncertain how much can be acquired in life's experiences. Obviously, Becky and Ruth had low empathy levels and had difficulty in thoughtfully considering their teachers' feelings in their decision making. When the two ladies made decisions that created widespread turmoil by treading on what Goleman terms "buried values," they displayed both a lack of self-awareness and a low level of empathy.

The two ladies also displayed extreme negative emotions and feelings that alienated and intimidated teachers. Judd demonstrated greater self-regulation (Goleman's term), but even he was accused of bristling and treating Sheila and Karen with disdain. Ruth was a classic case of a hot head in a Jekyll-and-Hyde costume who struck fear into the hearts of Wales's teachers.

Goleman's definition of "social skill" also has great relevance to the three cases. He sees social skills as being "friendliness with purpose." He is really talking about relationship building and the human relations skills that a leader must have in order to move people in the direction he desires. All three leaders lacked a high level of social skill and the ability as Goleman phrases it, "To find the common ground with people of all kinds."[15]

Goleman raises another point that is particularly significant to Becky's case. Becky was younger than Ruth and Judd with considerably less experience as a leader.

Southside was her "baptism of fire" as a school principal. Goleman[16] would claim that, with maturity as a leader, Becky will be capable of enhancing her emotional intelligence. He would refer to psychological and developmental research to support that notion.

Goleman would contend that Becky's failure at Southside could be a nurturing experience. It depends on how motivated she is to change and how receptive she is to feedback given. Will she be more empathetic, listen better, and be more self-regulated and self-aware in her next job? Will she acquire the social skills necessary to motivate others? One can only speculate.

As stated earlier, my experience separates me somewhat from Goleman's contention that emotional intelligence can be learned. I am less optimistic about the majority of school leaders being able to significantly elevate their emotional intelligence levels —especially older, experienced leaders, such as Ruth and Judd, who had records of past success.

I submit that Ruth and Judd don't necessarily have to radically change or acquire a range of higher emotional intelligence levels, except for a need to increase their self-awareness and self-regulation. They are above average in intelligence and possess the knowledge and skills to be effective leaders and are quite capable of learning from their Wales and Tremble experiences. Bitter failure is their best teacher. Hopefully, they will profit from their experiences having learned "the hard way." They also need to locate future positions where their leadership skills, needs, and values are a better organizational fit, thereby increasing their chances for success.

The English poet, John Keats, inspires us to profit from our mistakes and put it best when he wrote, "Failure is, in a sense, the highway to success, inasmuch as every discovery of what is false leads us to seek earnestly after what is true, and every fresh experience points out some form of error which we shall afterward carefully avoid."[17]

Fullan

Michael Fullan would fault the three leaders in several areas. First, he would criticize them for their impatience and their limited knowledge about the change process. He would remind them that effective change takes time and is "a process of development in use," whereas unrealistic timelines fail to recognize that implementation occurs developmentally. He would remind them that you cannot force or mandate change.[18]

He would tell them that no amount of knowledge will ever make it totally clear what action should be followed. There are no packaged solutions and instead refers to an effective leader as someone that has the ability to combine valid knowledge, political consideration, and make on-the-spot decisions and have intuition in making decisions.[19]

Fullan would therefore be critical of the one-dimensional, inflexible leadership approaches used by the three leaders. Becky's lack of experience limited her acquisition of knowledge and her lack of political wisdom could be explained. Her situation provided her with little basis for employing intuition and making quality on-the-spot decisions, particularly in a school where the faculty gave her little time and margin for error.

Although experienced in terms of years, Ruth and Judd had an established set of leadership behaviors that fit a specific situational context. Their leadership approach had worked well for them in their past situations. However, they were inexperienced in working and testing their leadership styles in different contexts and unfortunately assumed that "one size fits all." Tragically, they discovered that was not the case.

Finally, Fullan would criticize the leaders for rejecting shared decision-making approaches and for not following a consensus process that would result in greater commitments from those involved. He concludes that the proper visioning and planning "should occur only after administrators have acquired the necessary information, and have worked to build a climate supportive of collaboration."[20]

Judd tried to work collaboratively with the Tremble board in changing some lines of authority between him and the board. His failure was caused by his inability to convince them of the need for change, something that Fullan feels is essential to successful change.

Becky's initial problems, caused by a disgruntled staff that distrusted administrators, made it difficult for her to work collaboratively with teachers. Her authoritative style combined with some early mistakes related to her inexperience prevented consensus building. Instead, the "me against them" saga unfolded.

Ruth's inflexibility, stubbornness, and dogmatism created instant barriers to change. She had difficulty changing gears and controlling her emotions. She clearly did not take the time or have the patience to understand the culture of Wales, to convince the faculty and parents of the necessity for change, or to devise a thoughtful plan that would allow the staff to help shape and contribute to change.

Greenleaf and Others

Robert Greenleaf would question the leaders' failure to respect the competence of followers and work to make them even more competent and confident.[21] More contemporary authors on school leadership have recently expanded Greenleaf's servant leadership theories. Two of those authors are Joseph Rost and Thomas Sergiovanni.

Rost believes that followers do not do followership, they do leadership. He sees both leaders and followers forming one relationship that is leadership. They are the ones who initiate real change that reflect their mutual purposes. He compares the relationship to composers and musicians who do not do the same things in the relationship, but are both essential to leadership.[22]

Borrowing from Greenleaf, Sergiovanni in his work on moral leadership describes effective principals as servant leaders. These are leaders that command respect and followership of others, because they demonstrate dedication to the purposes of the organization and commitment to those who do the day-to-day tasks for those purposes to be realized. Similar to Rost's and Greenleaf's views, the school's needs are defined by shared values and purposes that Sergiovanni calls, the school's covenant. He envisions principals as ministers by providing leadership in a way that encourages others to be leaders.[23]

Becky and Ruth unquestionably did not act like servant leaders. Greenleaf, Rost, and Sergiovanni would claim that the two ladies and also the Tremble School Board reflect the traditional hierarchical bureaucracy. They would explain that in the three cases, leaders and followers do not have equal status with the values, commitments, vision, and covenants positioned at the top.

Sergiovanni maintains that there is a place for command leadership, instructional leadership, and interpersonal leadership, but the heart of one's leadership is one's ministerial role. Illustrations of this type of leadership are not present in any of the three case studies.

Judd's case provides little detail about his district-wide leadership. Instead, it concentrates mainly on his struggle to gain greater decision-making authority in order to enhance his command and interpersonal leadership. We can only speculate about his capacity to be a servant leader. His quick acceptance by teachers, parents, and community leaders suggest he had the skills if he had desired to establish a shared vision for his school district and include followers in conceptualizing and embracing that vision.

On the other hand, Judd's fixation in wanting greater role authority suggests he might simply have been interested in centralizing decision making in his office and was not really interested in working to establish shared covenants. Judd would disagree and claim that without the appropriate executive authority he would be incapable of delegating authority and sharing his power.

Becky's lack of professional maturity limited her vision of leadership. Conditions at Southside immediately forced her to use her position authority when challenged. At the time she began her duties, teachers did not want to follow her or any other administrator, for that matter. It would take an extremely long time for servant leadership to gain root in a school like Southside Elementary.

Ruth, however, did miss an opportunity to build consensus at Wales and work collaboratively with teachers. With a little nurturing of teachers, patience, anticipated staff turnover, central office support, teacher development, and the personal encouragement of a few capable teacher-leaders, successful change would have been possible—especially if the gracious and charming side of Ruth's personality became dominant. Unfortunately at this time in her career, Ruth was not open to or capable of ministering to Wales's teachers and building the necessary followership.

SUMMARY

Poor decisions made by search committees (note: the Tremble board was the only search committee for Judd), lack of administrative support, the inability and/or refusal to adapt leadership to new conditions, accepting new jobs for the wrong reasons, and limited breadth of experience, all contributed to the leadership failure of Becky Hazard, Ruth Maloney, and Judd Silva.

However, failure can teach us valuable lessons. The key is learning from our failures and in the process increasing our self-understanding. Hopefully, we will learn from our mistakes and gain the wisdom not to repeat them. Noted educational and corporate leadership writer Warren

Bennis says, "A true leader embraces their errors and realizes that most of us are shaped more by negative experiences than by positive ones."[24]

Educational leadership theorists offer considerable rationale on why school leaders fail and suggest pathways to successful leadership. Elevating one's emotional intelligence and practicing the principles of servant leadership are two recommendations.

The success of a school leader, however, really is dependent on two things: (1) the ability to adapt their leadership to different and/or changing situational contexts and (2) increasing self-understanding about their leadership strengths and weaknesses and making wise decisions by accepting new positions that are the best fit for them.

Not all leaders are inherently capable of transforming their leadership styles to fit certain contexts. Those who have the capacity to change will realize that such change will most likely take time, not occur overnight, and not always go smoothly. If they attempt to change, their success might also depend upon the degree of change required and what they have to sacrifice to adapt to new situations.

Then again, a school leader could be incapable of change or simply choose not to change his leadership style or image because it has worked well in the past. Judd and Ruth are two classic examples of leaders who refused to change their leadership approaches and, instead, chose to leave their positions and seek others where their style would be more acceptable.

In the final analysis, the ultimate choice rests with the school leader.

9

Helpful Tips for Hiring School Leaders

Before providing specific recommendations to prospective members of school executive search committees, it is important to briefly examine the several components of a search process. Recruitment, good assessment practices, search committee composition, hiring policies, and the development of job specifications are a few areas worth reviewing.

RECRUITMENT

Why school leaders fail is not an easy question to answer. With the unpredictability of human behavior, it is prudent to avoid pat answers to questions about how a person will react in a certain situation. Close friends who know a person well can't often predict with great reliability how that individual might cope under extreme pressure or conflict.

Recruitment firms will tell you that the best predictors for future performance of new executives are their prior experiences and interactions. They look for leaders that are the right fit for the organization's culture and have a genuine interest in the job opportunity.[25]

Recruitment, however, is not an exact science. Even with the compilation of considerable psychological and cognitive data on a candidate and careful alignment of that data with the organization's culture, an executive could fail badly in a new position. Good candidate assessment only lowers the odds that failure will be averted.

THE NEED FOR GOOD ASSESSMENT

Many school districts, for one reason or another, (cost, politics, ignorance) do not use search consultants. Although normally representative of the community, local search committees are usually unskilled in assessing the needs, goals, and values of a school organization and then identifying the type of leader best suited for that organization. They also receive little or no training before conducting a search.

The lack of a comprehensive assessment process sets in motion selection of candidates and a search process that could skew the data gathered. For example, data from reference checking, structured interviews, and candidate material requested for review might be unconnected to the organization's actual needs.

It also follows that huge mistakes can later be made by search committees in gathering and interpreting information on candidates. Most school districts do not use psychological or cognitive assessment tests, but rely on data solely from impressions gathered from interviews, reference checks, and, in some cases, site visits to the candidate's current school district. The use of role simulations, videotaping, candidate portfolios, and writing samples are used sparingly, but recently appear to be on the rise as candidate assessment tools.

Prior to the process used later during the interview stage, search committees should first determine the best procedures to be followed in advertising the vacancy and attracting the type of candidate that best matches the leadership profile identified through a careful assessment of the district's needs. Hopefully, they will then be searching for the right person.

SEARCH COMMITTEES

Principal and superintendent search committees usually function as screening committees appointed by the school board as advisory bodies. In many instances, lack of written board policy on selection procedures results in search committees becoming more than just advisory. In other cases, superintendents and boards shy away from set policies when they want greater control of the screening process. For example, the Tremble board assumed responsibility for the entire recruitment process when it hired Judd.

Furthermore, principal search committees can also include the superintendent, other central office administrators, or one or more school board members as voting members. In those instances, the superintendent and school board are involved in both the candidate screening and in the final selection process.

HIRING POLICIES

When hiring administrators, school board policies vary greatly. Human resource textbooks[26] call for written policies in a number of areas, including the application, interview, screening, and selection process. Other policies cover procedures for selection of search committees, internal and external recruitment procedures, responsibility for developing job specifications, and discrimination considerations in the application and interview process.

As previously mentioned, board hiring policies are generally not rigid in order to allow for shifts in board direction.

JOB SPECIFICATIONS

When job specifications are developed, the school board normally sets the parameters on salary, benefits, and length of contract. In some cases, negotiated contracts and state regulations influence decisions in these areas.

If a search consultant is hired, a process is adopted where other job requirements are fleshed out after data collection from surveys of parents, teachers and other school personnel, discussions with board members and the superintendent, and feedback solicited from the general public.

The search consultant then analyzes the data and prepares draft specifications for board approval. For example, after one community survey[27] of parents, teachers, and residents, 90% of the respondents stated they wanted a superintendent with the following characteristics that were later incorporated into the job specifications:

- demonstrated leadership skills
- knowledge of financial management
- knowledge of instructional and curricular issues
- experience in employee relations
- strong interpersonal skills

These extremely broad descriptions were approved by the school committee and incorporated into the application form, the position announcement, and a brochure. The job description was also forwarded to the search committee as a template to be used in their recruitment.

HELPFUL TIPS

The following suggestions are not meant to be overly critical of superintendents and school boards in the manner in which they recruit principals and superintendents. It is difficult to standardize recruitment policies because local politics, past history, finances, and demographics play major roles in determining the type of recruitment, selection, and retention policies used by different school districts.

The following "helpful tips" are therefore simply ideas that might lead to improving hiring practices in some school districts. I can say with certainty, however, that if the ideas had been utilized in the hiring of Becky, Ruth, and Judd, the odds of their not being hired would have risen dramatically and the odds of the right person being selected improved.

Although not meant to be an all-inclusive list, the following eleven tips are worthy of review before one accepts an invitation to serve on a search committee:

1. *The school board should provide sufficient funds to conduct a comprehensive search*
   The crucial importance of hiring the right school leader has to be acknowledged with a budget that allows for the hiring of a consultant and other forms of needed expertise. Failure of school boards to provide the necessary resources could result in a poor candidate selection and long-range costs, both financially and otherwise.

2. *Superintendents and board members should not sit on search committees*

As the board's chief executive officer, the superintendent's normal role in hiring district principals is to work closely with the search committee chair and keep the school board updated on committee developments. Having the superintendent and board members as voting members on the search committee is not only awkward but confuses the lines of authority and at times prevents objectivity in decision making.

3. *Search committee members should be trained*

Providing training to search committees prior to conducting a search is money well spent. The training does not have to be elaborate, but a trained consultant can provide an orientation to members on screening candidates, interviewing techniques, and collection of the type of data needed to make good decisions. For example, search committee members should know how to formulate the type of interview questions that will generate helpful data that, when added to the information base, will serve as reliable predictors of a candidate's future performance.

4. *Search committees should play a primary and not a secondary role in the development of job specifications*

After outlining its parameters in salary, benefits, and length of contract, the superintendent and school board should assist the search committee in generating data needed to develop comprehensive job specifications. If the board hires a search consultant, he should work closely with the search committee in finalizing a job description for superintendent and school board approval. By actually directly participating in conducting informational surveys, assessing organizational needs, and talking with key players, the search committee will gain important insights on the skills, qualities, and values preferred in the new school leader.

5. *Job specifications should be more than abbreviated, general statements*

Rather than a series of general statements (e.g., "the candidate will have high level interpersonal skills") more specific customized descriptions (e.g., "diffuse anger and find common ground to move people toward solutions") are needed to reflect a careful analysis of the culture and needs of the specific organization and the identification of the leadership that organization needs to be successful.

Surveys and small group feedback sessions with the superintendent and board members, district administrators, teachers, parents, and residents, along with school climate assessments done by outside agencies, are data sources to be used when designing more meaningful and focused "need descriptions."

One excellent example of a comprehensive leadership needs assessment is the selection criteria used in hiring urban principals by the New Leaders for Schools Project[28] in cities throughout the country.

New Leaders identifies three areas that are the basis for hiring strong leaders. Each area includes three to five descriptions. For example, "Communication and Listening" is followed by the descriptions (a) possess written and verbal skills to communicate with clarity, conciseness, and appropriateness to multiple audiences, (b) demonstrate poise and professionalism in diverse settings, (c) listen actively. In addition to the early descriptor about ability to diffuse anger, the category of "Interpersonal Skills" includes (a) build successful one-on-one relationships, (b) value each person's perspective and treat people with respect, (c) relate to adults and children: understand where they are going, what they need, and how to meet their needs, (d) exhibit confidence and competence under pressure.

It is interesting to reflect on how Becky, Ruth, and Judd would have been evaluated in these two categories. If their search committees had collected data from multiple sources as mentioned previously, and better understood the type of leadership that was more directly aligned with organizational needs, they may not have hired the three administrators. One also wonders if their failure to hire any form of consultant assistance was a fatal mistake.

Some search committees employ other approaches that are worthy of consideration. A recent trend is to have candidate interviews videotaped and structured around nationally recognized school leader standards, such as the Interstate School Leaders Consortium (ISLLC) standards, which have been research tested for reliability. Principal and superintendent candidates are now also required to take cognitive tests for certification in several states.[29]

6. *Serious consideration should to be given to assessment tools and selection techniques used by corporate America*

When a successful corporation hires a top executive, it usually first telephone screens candidates through a pre-assessment process[30] that utilizes structured questions in order to narrow the list of initial candidates.

If a candidate's profile in terms of experience and reference checks is also strong, a preliminary interview is conducted. If the company feels the candidate has considerable promise after the initial interview, the candidate is usually evaluated through an executive assessment. The process can be conducted online, in person by psychologists, or by an executive assessment center. Typically, the evaluation assesses emotional intelligence and cultural fit. It can measure more traditional functional assessments, such as leadership and communication style, personality traits, developmental needs, and potential blind spots. The data is then compared to a large sample of other domestic and global executives.

Once the evaluation is complete, the search committee then has the data to match the candidate to the most crucial competencies for the position.

For example, if the need is for a gregarious individual and team player rather than a creative thinker, then assessment norms will point that out. Another data point might be to assess how "tough a person's hide is." Does the candidate upset easily? What type of resiliency does s/he have? Is the candidate so sensitive that s/he personalizes most criticism? Data feedback on the three school leaders in these areas would have been invaluable to their search committees.

It is unusual for a company to call a candidate back for a second interview if she has not scored well on the cognitive and psychological assessment match criteria. If a second interview is conducted, the assessment data is invaluable to human resource people in shaping interview questions and indicating areas for further probing. The assessment tools greatly assist in improving the quality of interviews and in helping frame better questions when making final reference calls.

The goal is to match the candidate's skills and abilities with the uniqueness of the company's environment. Naturally, the ultimate goal is to get such a good match that high executive performance will result. Furthermore, a good match increases the odds of employee satisfaction, a condition that contributes to higher retention rates. The key is to generate as many data points from the assessment tools as possible, the objective being to get better employee quality by narrowing the degree of error. With sufficient data points, some firms claim that their assessment processes have an 80% success rate.[31]

Unfortunately, there is a tendency for educators to dismiss the use of assessment technology used in the corporate sector as expensive and unaffordable for financially strapped school districts.

One corporate human resource executive disagrees.[32] He contends that many online assessment programs need little customization to fit school executive assessment criteria.

Assuming that three finalists will make it to the final interview stage, he estimates an approximate cost of $200 for each assessment. Although admitting that recruitment is not a science and considerable subjectivity is still involved, he does view technology assessment data, when added to the myriad of data collected on a candidate from a variety of other sources, as a valuable tool in helping paint complete portraits of job finalists.

7. A reliable method for checking references beyond those submitted should be established

Relying solely on the opinions of references submitted by the candidate is a questionable practice. Reference calls to teachers, parents, and supervisors one or two jobs removed from a candidate's current position can reveal useful information. Gathering perceptions from persons that have worked with or for the candidate, as well as persons who have supervised the candidate can produce useful comparative data.

Although it is important to respect a candidate's wishes about not initially contacting current employers, every effort should be made to utilize other existing information networks to check on the candidate's qualifications and experience.

8. Recruiting highly qualified candidates should not be limited only to applications received

It is not the total number of candidates who apply for a leadership position that is important, but rather it is the number of highly qualified candidates who are in the applicant pool.

Although search committees may be reluctant to do so, they need to recruit highly qualified candidates by having a process in place, whereby they contact school leaders who might not have shown any interest in their vacancy, but who, when contacted and learn more about the job opportunity, will give it serious consideration. This responsibility should be left to a search consultant or the search committee chair if a consultant has not been hired.

Finding highly qualified candidates is the challenge. Recommendations should be sought from teachers, administrators, university professors, state education officials, executives in educational associations, and others who are in positions where they know of school leaders with outstanding reputations.

Although many will agree that there is a fine line between testing a potential candidate's interest in your vacancy and stealing talent from another school district, a professional approach to this type of active recruitment can be followed. Sending letters with recruitment materials to a prospective candidates, indicating they have been recommended for your vacancy is within ethical bounds. It is then the responsibility of the school leader to follow up the job opportunity or simply not respond. Asking the individuals who have sent letters recommending outstanding school leaders for the vacancy to place calls urging potential applicants to apply can lead to crossing the line.

9. *Both sides to the recruitment process should be considered*

A search process that is heavily weighted on compiling a comprehensive information base on a candidate often overlooks the candidate's need to receive reliable information on the position vacancy.

At least before, and definitely prior to a second interview, candidates should have accurate information about the challenges and current problems facing a new leader, the history of the school and school district, the nature and specific job expectations of people involved, and the current political and financial climate. School board policies and copies of recent board meeting minutes, accreditation reports, analyses of student achievement data, consultant studies are but a few examples of information that should be shared with the candidates.

Sufficient time should be scheduled for candidates to tour school facilities and meet with representative groups of teachers, parents, administrators, community leaders, and other constituents.

Wise candidates also conduct their own research utilizing their contacts to gather information on the community and its schools. Reading past copies of the local newspaper and informally touring the community and talking with local patrons in the town coffee shop as inconspicuously as possible often provide a candidate with valuable information.

The importance of a candidate having a thorough understanding of the job vacancy before he accepts a job offer cannot be stressed enough. Failure to do so can create serious problems in the future. Just ask Judd Silva.

10. *The staff and community should be engaged in the search process*

Although sometimes cumbersome and time consuming, having the staff and community actively participate in the search provides additional perspectives and insights about the candidate that are sometimes missed by search committees.

A well-organized public forum where staff and interested residents ask candidates questions enables search committees to get written and structured feedback that can be summarized and added to the candidate's information base.

Public forums also allow the search committee, board, and superin tendent to observe how well a candidate presents himself before a large audience. After all, school leaders are public figures and must present appropriate public images. How articulate is the candidate? How knowledgeable does the candidate appear? How poised is the candidate when difficult questions are posed by difficult people? How does the candidate respond when he doesn't have an answer? Does his body language give him away? Do you think the audience likes him? Why? Getting these simple impressions from the general public can be invaluable to a search committee.

Although welcome at the public forum, teachers and other school staff need a separate place and time to meet with principal and superin tendent candidates to ask their in-depth questions and gather impressions they can forward to the search committee.

11. *Search committees should forward their recommendations to the board regarding any special circumstances prior to finalist selection*

After completing their assignment and forwarding the names of finalists to the school board, search committees should personally share their findings in a special meeting.

Following their overview of the finalist candidates, the search members need to share information they have gathered on nuances of certain problems that might be unknown to board members and even the superintendent. For example, the problems at the Southside School were not going to disappear with the appointment of Becky Hazard or any other principal appointee. The need for greater clarity and planning on the role the superintendent would play in Becky's induction was crucial.

The need for an outside mentor for Becky was a particular concern and the search committee had a responsibility to bring this crucial need to the superintendent's and board's immediate attention. Other changes, particularly reassignment of some Southside faculty and staff prior to a new principal's arrival at Southside, also deserved serious consideration. Did the search committee make these recommendations? Unlikely, given the search process followed. If they did make such recommendations, why did the superintendent and board ignore them? It is too bad these actions were not taken because future bloodshed might have been avoided.

SUMMARY

Search committees that lack training, operate with limited budgets, and do not have the services of a consultant are at a disadvantage. This lack of support and role preparation can lead to bad selection decisions.

Helpful tips for search committees to improve their decision making are the use of technology assessment tools in order to expand their information base, adopting measures to actively recruit talented leaders, and ensuring that prospective candidates have sufficient information about the specific challenges the position presents before they accept a job offer.

An underlying theme is to convince school boards and their search committees of the need to generate more reliable data on candidates and avoid the current overreliance on impressions created by candidates in interviews and in reference checks. Increased information aligned with the leadership needs of the organization will reduce the margin for error in decision making.

Public forums, writing samples, structured interviews, visitations to a finalist candidate's current school district, reflective portfolios, and other data-gathering activities add important data to the information base on a candidate. However, a careful analysis of the leadership needs of the organization followed with candidate data from cognitive and psychological assessments tests will increase the chances of getting a good match of the leader with the position vacancy. The greater the match, the more it becomes a win-win situation for both the school leader and the school district.

In closing, I cannot guarantee that Becky Hazard, Ruth Maloney, and Judd Smith would have survived if the search committees described in the three cases in this book had followed the advice presented in the eleven "tips." With more relevant information, would the committees have made different decisions? Would having more details and a better feel for the challenges awaiting them have caused the three leaders to pause and decline these new positions? Who knows? Even if the three leaders still took the positions, they might have had more insight, and have done things differently, and spared themselves some pain and anguish. Were they simply poor matches for the organizations they were asked to lead?

In the final analysis, blame for failure must extend beyond the three school leaders. Many people contributed to their failure; unfortunately, it was the three school leaders who paid the heaviest price.

Acknowledgments

I am indebted to Becky Hazard, Ruth Maloney, Judd Silva, and others appearing in the three case studies for sharing their stories and opinions with me. Their real names remain anonymous. I apologize if I have upset anyone by stating opinions or have manipulated, misunderstood, or fictionalized some facts. My primary intent is to learn from these unfortunate situations and to keep others from making the same mistakes.

Becky, Ruth, and Judd recovered nicely from these low points in their careers. They are stronger, more insightful, and better prepared to face new challenges. I wish them well.

My thanks also go to the hundreds of graduate students I have taught during the past two decades. As people preparing to become new principals and superintendents, they have provided me with the opportunity to share in their dreams, their disappointments, and their victories. I have learned much from them and hopefully they have profited from working with me in becoming effective school leaders. I need to unequivocally state that an overwhelming majority of these students are very successful administrators and are having a very positive impact on the lives of their students.

In forty-three years in public education, I have known many principals and superintendents who have shared their trials and tribulations with me. Their contributions are reflected in my thinking and writing.

As a school superintendent for eighteen years, I worked directly with a number of principals, some superb and others mediocre. Each and every one taught me something useful.

Finally, I would like to thank Judy Robinson, a teacher friend from my distant past, for helping me with the editing of this book, assistance I desperately needed. My thanks also go to my son, Kevin, for his corporate expertise and the information he provided in the area of executive recruitment, selection, and retention, and to my daughter-in-law, Katie Holland, for her technology assistance in reformatting my ever-changing manuscript.

My thanks to all who have contributed to this book. I am much in your debt.

Sources

1. Daniel Goleman, "What Makes a Leader?" *Harvard Business Review*, 1998, pp. 93–102.

2. Michael Fullan, "Leadership for the 21st Century, Breaking the Bonds of Dependency," *Educational Leadership*, Vol. 55, No.7, 1998, pp. 1–3.

3. Robert Greenleaf, *Teacher as Servant*, New York: Paulist Press, 1977.
Greenleaf's concept of servant leadership has been used extensively by other educational authors in recent years—especially Thomas Sergiovanni when he writes about moral leadership and principals "ministering to the needs of the schools they serve.

4. The self-assessment was a component of the president's performance evaluation prepared for his board's review. Excerpts are summarized with the permission of the president.

5. W. Edwards Deming, *Out of Crisis*, MIT/CAES, 1986. See Deming's 14 points in Chapter 2.

6. Thomas J. Sergiovanni, *The Principalship: A Reflective Practice Perspective*, Allyn and Bacon, 1995, pp. 99–123.
Sergiovanni's chapter on the forces of leadership includes descriptions of the principal as technical leader, as human leader, as educational leader, as symbolic leader, and as cultural leader.

7. T. B. Greenfield, *Leaders and Schools: Willfullness and Non-Natural Order in Organizations*. In T.F. Sergiovanni and J.E. Corbally (eds.) *Leadership and Organizational Culture*. Urbana:University Press, 1984, pp. 142–169.

8. H. Brinker, "Strategic Planning Forward in Reverse," *Harvard Business Review*, November, 1984. Brinker defines vision as being a compass that allows people to buy in and take part in shaping the school's mission. Years later, certifi-

cation and educational leadership accreditation standards included definitive statements about the school leader establishing and sharing a vision for his school. See the Interstate School Leaders Consortium (ISLLC) Standards, Council of Chief School Officers, Washington D. C., 1996. Also see Susan More Johnson's chapter on crafting a vision in her book, *Leading to Change: The Challenge of the New Superintendency*, San Franciso: Jossey-Bass Publishers, 1996, pp. 61–90.

9. The "hammer and the velvet glove" reference made by Ethel Briggs does not appear in any of Hemmingway's novels. Ethel was quoting something she read about the style of Hemmingway's writing, not actually quoting any of his novels.

10. Trevanian, *Shibumi*, New York: Ballantine Books, 1979, p. 105.

11. Goleman, op. cit., pp. 93–94.

12. Ibid., pp. 95–95.

13. Ibid., p. 97.

Goleman offers an interesting explanation of how both nurture and genetics play a role in emotional intelligence. He also cites research indicating that emotional intelligence is born largely in the neuro-transmitters of the brain's limbic system.

14. Ibid., pp. 101–102.

15. Ibid., p. 102.

Goleman is certain that emotional intelligence increases with age. Although even with maturity, he admits some people still need training to enhance their emotional intelligence.

16. John Keats, English poet (1795–1821) from *The New Dictionary of Thoughts: A Cyclopedia of Quotations*, edited by Tryron Edwards, Standard Book Company, 1957, p. 197.

17. Michael Fullan, *Change Forces*, London: Falmer Press, 1993, p. 40.

The three school leaders should read Fullan's eight basic lessons of the new paradigm of change found where he writes about the "dynamic complexity" of change and provides insights on the change process.

18. Michael Fullan, *The Meaning of Change*, New York: Teachers College Press, 1982, pp. 91–92.

19. Fullan, op.cit., pp.17–18.

Fullan discusses how collaboration is essential for personal learning and how people need one another to accomplish things.

20. Greenleaf, op.cit.

21. Joseph C. Rost, *Leadership for the Twenty-First Century*, Westport, CT: Praeger Publishers, 1993, pp. 107–112.

22. Sergiovanni, op.cit., pp. 334–334.

23. Warren Bennis, *On Becoming a Leader*, Reading, MA:Addison-Wesley, 1989, p. 18.

24. From Caliber Associates, an executive search firm with offices in Wayne, Pennsylvania and San Diego, California. This information was found on their Web site, caliberassociates.com.

25. See William B. Castetter, *The Human Resource Function in Educational Administration*, 6th edition, Englewood Cliffs, NJ: Prentice Hall, 1996, pp. 85–123.

26. Survey results reported on Web site of Pocantico Hills Central School District Board of Education, Sleepy Hollow, NY, December, 2005.

27. New Leaders for New Schools, National Program Office, 30 West 26th Street, New York, NY.

New Leaders aggressively recruits nationwide, seeking talented people to become urban school principals. Urban principals are hired for Memphis, Baltimore, New York City, Chicago, and the California Bay area. Information cited is from selection criteria listed on their Web site.

28. *Interstate School Leaders Consortium (ISLLC) Standards*, Council of Chief School Officers, Washington, D.C. 1996.

By 1999, 18 states had adopted the ISLLC standards. In 2001, a consortium of national education associations joined to promote acceptance of the standards in all 50 states and in Washington D.C. and worked with Educational Testing Service to develop an assessment tool. The growing national trend has seen ISLLC standards become the basis for educational leadership state program approval, for state principal and superintendent certification, for hiring and induction of new administrators, and as an appraisal tool for administrative performance.

29. Information on corporate executive searches was gathered in an interview with Kevin Holland, currently senior executive vice president of human resources for Chiquita.

30. Tim McGonigle of Caliber Associates does job analyses and test development and validating products for a variety of occupations. In an assessment process developed with Coors, the company achieved an 87% success rate.

31. Holland contends that the use of assessment technology is cost effective and would be a valuable addition to the school executive assessment process. Other search firms using assessment technology are Valtera Corporation of Chicago and Personnel Decisions International (PDI) with global headquarters in Minneapolis. These firms employ teams of psychologists who are skilled in assessment technology and, as PDI advertises on its Web site, "Helps select leaders who drive results and gain advantage in the competitive world."

About the Author

Dr. William Holland is professor emeritus of Educational Leadership at Rhode Island College in Providence, Rhode Island. After beginning as a junior high school English and social studies teacher in Newton, Massachusetts, Holland served as an assistant principal and assistant superintendent for four years before spending the next eighteen years in both Massachusetts and Rhode Island as a school superintendent in three different school districts. In 1988, Dr. Holland was appointed as professor at Rhode Island College, where he served as department chair and taught courses in educational leadership in the master's, advanced degree, and doctoral programs for seventeen years. From 1989 through 1999, he was executive director of the Rhode Island Association of School Principals. From 1999 through 2002, Dr. Holland served as Rhode Island Commissioner for Higher Education. Currently, he is active as an educational consultant.